Madon

Why Men Are Wired To Cheat On Women!

Peter Andrew Sacco Ph.D.
&
Debra Laino D.H.S.

chipmunkapublishing
the mental health publisher

Peter Andrew Sacco Ph.D. & Debra Laino D.H.S.

Published by

Chipmunkapublishing

PO Box 6872

Brentwood

Essex CM13 1ZT

United Kingdom

http://www.chipmunkapublishing.com

Copyright ©
Peter Andrew Sacco Ph.D. & Debra Laino D.H.S. 2011

ISBN 978-1-84991-629-5

Chipmunkapublishing gratefully acknowledge the support of Arts Council England.

ACKNOWLEDGMENTS

When you ask people if they know what the Madonna complex is, they usually squint at you and respond, "Say what?". The quickly they nod and say something like, "Oh, you mean that singer who was once married to Sean Penn and sings *Like A Virgin*!" And this is when we would say something like, "Yeah right...you don't know, do you?".

We would like to thank all of those who had the patience to listen to us and respond to our questions. Yes, some of our interviews were excruciatingly long! We are very grateful for those willing to share their personal stories and case studies with us.

We would like to thank all of the great psychologists, psychiatrists, sociologists and researchers who contributed their efforts into generating insights into what the Madonna-whore complex was and is today.

Thank you to our readers. We hope this book helps you understand your own situation or others better!

DEDICATION

This book is dedicated to anyone who struggles with an addiction or mental health problem. We also dedicate it to those living with those who have addiction and mental health problems and support your loved ones.

We would also like to dedicate this book to all of those who supported us in making this book a reality.

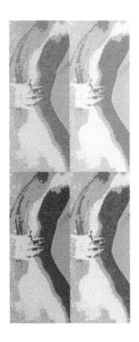

Peter Andrew Sacco Ph.D. & Debra Laino D.H.S.

CHAPTERS

*All of the case studies in this book were contributed to us by those willing to be interviewed. These individuals did not receive any monetary rewards for sharing any personal experiences with us. We did change their names to protect their anonymity.

FORWARD

I have always wondered how far some people will go to please the people they work with, or get ahead in their careers. As I write this, I am in the process of looking for a new job as I just resigned from my well-paying job. You know what? I feel great!

I worked as an executive assistant for a marketing firm. I was with the same company for 3 years. In the beginning I really loved coming to work. The people I worked with were great. Perhaps it was their habits which led me to quit. You see, many of our meetings were settled over drinks and steak. Well, that was until the last year and a bit when they were being worked out over drinks, steak and naked women. Yes, going to the strip clubs once or twice a week had become the business norm. It became a good ole boys club. If you didn't tag along and participate in their fun, then you were never destined to advance and become an associate.

I played the game and went to the "ballet" as they eloquently referred to it as. I must admit, that after the first couple of visits which I felt shameful and out of place were under my belt, I actually started enjoying my time there. I wasn't much of a drinker, even in my younger years. And I still am not much of a drinker today. I have been married for twelve years and it's been a fairly stable marriage. We have a 9 year old daughter and 5 year old son. It's funny, but it took going to the "ballet" to appreciate my wife and children that much more.

You see, it all came to me one morning sitting across from my daughter at the breakfast table. I was getting so wound up looking at naked women that I lost sight of real beauty. The shame I originally had walking into the strip clubs changed to anticipation, excitement and arousal. I had become so desensitized to watching naked women, I forgot to see a female for what she was. As I looked across at my daughter, I thought about the girls working at the club. Those women belonged to someone. They were someone's daughter, sister or mother. What if that was my daughter up there one day? A sharp chill raced up my spine sending shock-waves to my brain. What had I become? Who was this face now looking back at me from across the room in the glass cupboards? I was disgusted by my own reflection!

Business would always be handled the same way at the firm. However, the way I was handling myself was less than admirable and I had to do something about it soon. I wanted to be in the strip club too much. What if I became addicted to it? I remember counting in my head how many times I had been there the last month. It made me nauseated.

Sexual intimacy with my wife never happened anymore. I couldn't have sex with her because I was cheating on her, at least in my mind I was. Eventually I started sleeping on the couch every night as I didn't want to contaminate her, or have her read my racing thoughts.

In fact, I worried I would talk in my sleep thus revealing I was frequenting strip clubs as well as using the Internet to find porn sites to satisfy my sexual addictions. The funny part was I was not having sex with anyone, including my wife!

The day finally came when the truth came out. I couldn't live with myself or how I was acting so I told my wife in private what was happening to me. Fearing she would leave me, I prepared to pack some things together and find a motel. Instead she embraced me and told me she would do whatever it took to save our marriage.

I quit my job because I really believed I was playing for the wrong team. The team that comes first is my family and I can't compromise what I have in the name of a bigger pay check, some cheap thrills and trying to be accepted by my peers.

I sought help for my sex addiction and currently consider myself in recovery. Even though thoughts of sex with other women occasionally flicker into my mind, I quickly distract myself or remove them from my thinking.

Sex addictions are real! Sex addictions can destroy a person! I am very grateful to have been asked to review this book before it went to publication. I feel that both Peter and Debra have done a marvelous job in describing the Madonna Complex and sex addiction. Everything they talk about is right on. In many areas of the book, reading it was like rehashing my own life!

If you are struggling with sex addiction or porn addiction, it doesn't matter whether you are man or woman, or if you know someone close to you who has these type of addictions, then this book is for you. To date I have not read a more insightful and informative book on something that not too many people know about or talk about.

I hope this book leads you to recognize that help is out there and that there are better choices you can make for your life. This book should be a staple read for any sex addiction group or co-dependency group!

As I close, it feels good to be my own person again. Best of all, I feel like a complete man again and I wish you peace and joy in your own life! Thank you Peter and Debra for writing this exceptional book!

SCOTT W.

INTRODUCTION

To be brave is to love someone unconditionally, without expecting anything in return. To just give. That takes courage; because we don't want to fall on our faces or leave ourselves open to hurt.

Madonna

If you ask anyone on the street, in a shopping mall or bar, "Have you ever heard of the Madonna complex?" they are usually quick to answer something like..."Isn't that about 'that girl', you know the provocative chick from the 1980's who sang *Like A Virgin*?" Often times the responses you get are closely tied to one Madonna Louise Ciccone, singer, dancer, actress extraordinaire! Guess what? The Madonna complex has nothing to do with Madonna the entertainer, nor does it have anything to do with the Blessed Mother Mary. So, what is it then, and where the heck did this ubiquitous concept come from?

We're sure you already have a lot of questions about this "complex" and who, what, where, why and when did it come from. Amongst those questions, we're sure you also have the "how" in your back pocket, ready to throw out any moment--How does it work and how does it affect people? We will definitely get around to answering those questions as well! And we're sure there will be many other questions and particular curiosities we hope to engage the reader in throughout this book.

The goal of this book is to enlighten and educate readers about the Madonna complex. We want to make this book as reader-friendly as possible. Each chapter will provide working definitions and insights into the Madonna complex and contain case studies and examples characteristic of various aspects of the complex.

Before you start reading this book, we would like you to ponder the following questions. Perhaps this will prime your thought processes as well as the values you possess toward the intricacies of the complex which you will read about in this book.

1) Do you believe that relationships and marriages were created/formed for the purpose of ensuring monogamy?

2) Do you believe in monogamy?

3) Do you believe polygamy is okay/acceptable if all parties involved in whatever kind of relationship they are in are okay with it?

4) Do you believe people can become addicted to sex?

5) Do you believe people can become addicted to relationships and/or other people?

6) Do you believe that in this day/age the media still places too much emphasis on sex and lust?

7) Do you believe viewing pornography can lead to promiscuity and/or sex addictions?

8) Do you believe that people already possessing sex addiction or have an addictive personality seek out pornography because they can relate to it at a level they are wired into?

9) Do you believe the institute of marriage, even relationships are held as sacred today as they once were?

10) Do you believe it is possible for a person to be with and remain with the same partner "forever"?

11) Do you hold to the stereotype that men are more likely to be cheaters than women?

12) Do you believe women are still held to a standard of being sexually reserved?

13) Do you believe sex is still a taboo subject that should not be expressed or discussed openly in public?

14) Do you think television shows and sex education classes geared toward children now at an earlier age lead to increased sexual promiscuity/behaviors later in life?

15) Do you believe that in today's day/age almost anything "goes" sexually as long as all involved are willing and/or consenting?

16) Do you think people are still prudish about sex in Western society...it's dirty, disgusting and shameful to express or expose the human body?

17) Do you believe technology, especially the Internet has led to an increase in sexual promiscuity, infidelity and divorce rates?

18) Do you think that once someone "cheats" on their spouse they are always a cheater?

19) Do you think if society restored the institute of marriage and made it difficult to get divorces, while at the same time banning common-law marriages that infidelity would decrease?

20) Do you know of someone who believes, or do you believe women are inferior to men and were created to serve men and bear children?

Now keep in mind there are no right or wrong answers to these questions, then again that all depends who you ask and who is listening! The purpose of reading through these questions is for you to question, challenge and explore the beliefs you currently hold about relationships and sex.

We're sure that some of the questions you have just read may have provoked feelings of shock and disdain. Interestingly, there are many individuals who actually condone and subscribe to some of the activities

Peter Andrew Sacco Ph.D. & Debra Laino D.H.S.

and subject matter within these questions--Whatever floats some peoples' boats so to speak! Coincidentally, those sailing these same vessels are collecting water so fast that their ships (relationships/lives) are sinking like the Titanic!

Even though society and media teaches that "Everyone is doing it!", "Variety is the spice of life!", or "It's destined to be the societal norm!", does not make it right or healthy for individuals, and relationships as a whole. What often gets left out of the mix is the degree of damage done to the human psyche!

Human beings are social creatures. They are definitely sexual beings as well. It is very important to realize that underneath the exterior is human spirit. There is no doubt society is at an all-time high in terms of relationship dysfunction/divorce, mental health issues, and the overall breakdown of the family and the values it once held sacred. If ever there was one cure that was almost guaranteed to work and "fix" people, it is to get in touch with their inner selves--their spirit! Somewhere along the way too many people got caught up in the "sexuality" illusion...if it feels good, then just do it! Kind of sounds like a sexual lubricant commercial combined with a running shoe advertisement! Some people literally think with what is below the waist and not with what is in their heads or hearts...their spirit. Today it seems human spirit has become compromised by human libido. Who would have thought Freud's assertions of the life instinct (the striving for sexual gratification) from the 1800's would be so prevalent in today's society? It truly makes you wonder how far we've really evolved mentally, emotionally and spiritually over the last two centuries.

At the end of the day, for each person their reality is truly a state of their own minds...their perceptions. So many people are living in distorted realities with delusional thinking and perhaps the reality of their current lifestyles versus what they pretend them

to be are definitely figments of their imaginations. Wouldn't it be great if and when the majority could start imagining and living healthy relationships?
Stay tuned!

CHAPTER ONE

**WHAT IS THE
MADONNA
COMPLEX?**

**"The art of procreation and the members employed
therein are so repulsive, that if it were not for the beauty
of the faces and the adornments of the actors and the
pent-up impulse, nature would lose the human species."**

Leonardo daVinci

The Madonna complex is commonly referred to and known as the Madonna-whore complex. Rather than referring to the complex in harsh terms each time we mention it, we decided to leave out the "whore" part and simplify it as the Madonna complex.

The Madonna complex is not some catchy "pop" psychology concept which sprung roots over night. As a matter of fact, its roots go all the way back to Sigmund Freud and his psychosexual theories. Freud was a major believer in the notion that all human behaviour -- wishes, dreams and gratifications, had a strong psychosexual basis. Moreover, Freud was often times accused of hanging onto perverse theories of personality development.

One of the theories Freud is best known for is his 5 stages of psycho-sexual development:

STAGE ONE ORAL

STAGE TWO ANAL

STAGE THREE PHALLIC

STAGE FOUR LATENT

STAGE FIVE GENITAL

Freud's first stage, *ORAL* is the stage when infants learn to perceive and experience the world through their mouths. They cry, they feed, they teethe, they burp, and they cry for help. The power they exert over their lives comes from their "oral abilities".

The *ANAL* stage still occurs in infancy, babies and toddlers (2-3 year olds) learn to exert a degree of control over their lives through sensations they experience in their anus. When we refer to the anus we are not splitting hairs here and giving you a figurative metaphor. We are talking buttocks, derriere, bum ... ass! Children become interested and amused with the sensations of holding their excrement in or letting it out. They exert control over those around them by deciding when and where they decide to go to the washroom. Days require planned time and/or delays over their child going potty or going in their pants. Things often get messy and time consuming. Interestingly, children learn they can control their parents' time by holding it in or letting it out!

The *PHALLIC* stage according to most psychoanalysts and Freud, is the time when literally everything starts to happen in the child's life. The *Oedipus Complex* in boys and the *Electra Complex* in girls, define associations and relationships with the parents. Gender identity and gender concept also start to occur at this age. Many boys and girls in early childhood actually start playing show and tell with body parts. Boys learn that it's cool to be a boy because they have a penis. Some boys also experience castration anxiety because of this same penis! Girls on the other hand wish they had a penis. They wish they could be boys. They suffer from penis envy!

The *LATENT* Stage is a period of latency. Sexual energies and perceptions are dormant. Nothing is happening. Children are encouraged to be children and play. Boys do boy stuff and girls do girl stuff. Everything is status quo!

Finally the *GENITAL* stage is basically what it advertises itself to be. According to Freud, this is the period during puberty leading onward where individuals identify their sexual orientation, ex., heterosexual, homosexual, bi-sexual. They also start to experiment with sex and to develop and understand intimacy.

In a nut shell, these are **Freud's 5 Psychosexual Stages**. Freud believed individuals could become fixated at any one stage which would hinder their personality development. If they never resolved these childhood issues, they would always persist into their teenage years and adult lives.

It is during stage three, the *PHALLIC STAGE*, that we find the seeds of the Madonna complex. Freud believed the mother was the parent who had the ability to have the greatest impact on her son's life in terms of dysfunctional psychosexual development. As a matter of fact, less than one hundred years later, famous movie director Alfred Hitchcock saw the brilliance in Freud's theory and created the cinematic horror masterpiece Psycho, a story about Norman Bates' perverse love for his mother and his dysfunctional appreciation of women. Hitchcock demonstrated how a son can turn psychopathic toward his mother and women as a result of a faulty Oedipus Complex perpetuated by fixation and dissolution in the Phallic stage of Psychosexual development. Of course this was only a movie and many men grow up having dysfunctional relationships with their mothers but they do not graduate into becoming sociopaths and serial killers. Other negative attributes resulting from dysfunctional development during this psychosexual stage rear their ugly heads in the formation, creation and maintaining of relationships with women.

Freud also believed in what he called the Life instinct. Freud believed in evolution and spreading/sowing seeds to keep a species going. He believed humans, like animals, cannot, or have tremendous difficulty, remaining monogamous. Moreover, this is the case for men. He believed men had a built-in (innate) mechanism which encouraged them to be highly active sexual creatures. Something in them drives them to "sew their seeds" and have as much sex as possible with as many different women. Imagine Freud being your psychiatrist doing couples counselling? One can only imagine uncontrollable "seed sewing" being offered up as the reason for a husband cheating on his wife!

The life instinct asserts that men are extremely sexual beings, always on the lookout for "something" appealing or better than what they have. Of course this "something" is strongly rooted in the visual domain -- sex in the media, provocative dressed women and places where "sex sells" (strip clubs, bars, massage parlours, etc.). According to Freud's belief system, men can't help themselves from looking... They try on other women for size!

DAVE'S PERCEPTION OF POWER - A CASE STUDY

From the time I was a kid it is very safe to say I was glad I was not a girl. Very glad! I am in my late 30's now and you know what? I am still glad I am a man and not a woman!

Back in the day I came from a small family, myself and a brother and a sister. We were raised the southern part of the USA. As a kid, I saw how my mother was treated by my father and deep down I knew something wasn't right. He treated her like crap, a second rate person. He also treated my sister like that too. He never treated my brother or me like that. My brother and I were both jock-types and played football and competed on other varsity teams throughout high school and then college. My father not only encouraged us, but in some ways worshipped the ground my brother and I walked on. My father had always wanted to play pro football but got my mother pregnant before he was out of high school. His dream of football was over at that point. I think he partially blamed her for that!

Getting back to women being treated as second class, I also saw it in the community I was raised in. It seemed women were there to cook, clean and make babies. And when they weren't doing any of these three things, they were waiting to take orders on other things from their husbands, or men they were around. Who would want to be a woman with this type of treatment?

I am married with my own kids. To be honest I sucked at relationships when I was younger. I got dumped a lot because women found me "rude". It wasn't until I met the woman I am married to now that she set me straight on a few things -- namely learning to treat women better. Looking back I saw how wrong my father was to my mother and my sister. Is it any wonder that my sister moved away and never came back? And to this day, my parents are still married and my father still puts my mother down, even though it isn't as bad, as he seemed to have mellowed out over the years. With that said, I am still glad I wasn't born a woman. I could see it was hard then, and I think it is still probably hard to be a woman in this world!

The life instinct is strongly based on Freud's belief in evolution. He believed that all species, even humans, are extremely competitive by their innate natures and compete (need) to produce offspring. If you look at society as a whole, today it is still very male-dominated with men holding the highest positions, earning the most money and ruling the roost. Men have been, are and always will be in competition with one another as that is the order of the human universe.

Ever wonder where the term "notch in one's belt" came from? This has a very strong connotation to men conquering and exploiting women. The more the better! Back in the day, and it certainly still happens today, some men compete to see who can have sex with the most women. This is all based on power derived from playing the game... Competition! If you delve further into this assertion, then it is strongly based on male ego -- male dominance. By the way, the concept *"EGO"* is also another one of Freud's components of personality (*ID, EGO and SUPEREGO*). Ironically Freud was the architect behind the theory of "PENIS ENVY". Freud postulated women possessed an "envy" if you will for the male phallic because of what it could do and what it stood for, no pun intended!

Literally speaking, it allowed men a certain kind of power because they could "pee" standing up, as well as outside behind a tree. Figuratively speaking, the society at the time Freud lived in, was highly male dominated and women were often viewed as second class citizens. Therefore, it was much better to be a man. Because of your "penis", you possessed greater power and... You could pee standing up! Interestingly, in our book *PENIS ENVY: DOES SIZE REALLY MATTER OR IS IT THE SIZE OF THE MATTER?* we took Freud's penis envy and applied it to this day/age, together with a big twist to the theory. What we did was, we applied it to men! We showed how men are in "stiff" competition with one another in many areas of their lives and feel the need to constantly keep up with their gender-related peers and referent power holders. Who would have thought a male psychiatrist who created a theory about a penis applicable toward women would see it come full circle and be applied to men -- the ones who actually own the penis?

It is this penis envy which men foster/capitulate in their own lives today that has a bearing on keeping up with other guys and adding notches on their gunfighter belts.

If the whole notion of "reversed penis envy" wasn't bad enough, men competing with men, then the whole notion of men competing with women has become yet another can of worms leading to the Madonna complex. For the most part, in today's western world both genders are on an evening playing field in terms of equality... Or so we would like to think. Wage disparities and career opportunities have narrowed between men and women making both genders equal in the work world. Furthermore in some societies, affirmative action, where women were given preference to jobs and careers over men to try to balance things out, became a trend -- a temporary experiment.

What it did to some men was create anxiety, fear and inferiority complexes! Remember, men were always the referent power holders in the real world, the bread winners. Women came a long way which in essence took forever, but came to power in a period of time at an accelerated rate leaving some men blinded with whiplash. This couldn't have been too appealing to men, especially those who always possessed power or came from pedigree where power was passed onto them in careers like law, medicine, policing, construction work, military, professional sports, etc. In the blink of an eye, the perception and reality of male power and dominance was taken away. How in the world could men cope with this?

The Madonna complex or meaningless sex with women, compensated, massaged and titillated the male ego. The sex served as a pacifier for power -- it demonstrated to some men that they could love them and leave them. Women may "have come a long way baby", but not in the bedroom, or in the rules of love. Many men still perceive themselves as the referent power holders in this domain.

Often times the issue has arisen, "Why are so many men afraid of commitment?" The rhetorical question could be asked, "Why buy the cow when they can get the milk for free?" Is it really a commitment issue or is it men using women and exerting a distorted perception of power which they think they hold? In essence, some men use women whether they do so consciously or unconsciously.

Some men use women sexually not only in order to build up their own egos through their perceived ability to control them, but also do so because they are angry with women in general. Exploitation through sex is a means some men use to get even with women. Moreover the women they use for sex are representative of the women who have hurt them in the past through neglect or rejection.

Research in mother-infant attachments/bonding show that within the first year of a baby's life, the attachment they have to their mothers is extremely important, especially in forming secure relationships later in life. This early relationship between mother and son is extremely important for how men treat women and form relationships with them. Obviously, men who had ambivalent, anxious, disorganized or disoriented relationships with their mothers as babies/children are more likely to form carbon copy relationships with the women they meet. In fact, many will seek out psychological replicas of their mothers -- they look to meet women who remind them of their mothers consciously or unconsciously. David Celani the author of *The Illusion of Love* discusses the relationships people form based on *Object Relations Theory*. Celani incorporates a strong Psychoanalytical theme model based on Freud's attachment theories. Without summarizing the Celani's book (we highly recommend reading it), *Object Relations Theory* asserts individuals seek out relationship partners who best represent their opposite sex parent. Of course the playing field gets slightly altered in gay/lesbian relationships, which of course you are less likely to find the Madonna complex occurring -- that is unless the husband in a heterosexual marriage is having sex on the side with and only with, another man. That's another book altogether!

MEASURING UP - A CASE STUDY

I am a 29 year old man who is addicted to masturbation. When most people think about addictions, they will quickly turn their minds to things like alcohol, drugs, gambling or eating. You sometimes hear about people with sex addiction in the media -- this usually after they have been busted screwing around on their wives. I don't have a wife and I don't even have a girlfriend. When I did have a girlfriend in the past (2 years ago) she dumped me because there was no sex in our relationship. She wanted to and I wanted to as well, but when we did it, I could never get satisfied (I never ejaculated and actually did not want to because I worried about getting her pregnant. What would happen if someone "better" came along and I was stuck with her?). After a while she stopped trying to have sex with me. In fact, she stopped asking for it!

There was no doubt in my mind she probably cheated on me the nearly 2 years we were together. There was a part of me that even wanted that as long as I could "have" her for companionship. I just really wanted someone like her to have as a mate. When it came to sex, I wanted to have sex with the women I fantasized about most!

I watched a lot of porn at night on Direct TV channels and Internet. Since we never lived together I would watch it after she went home or I left her apartment. Some nights I would tell her I was very tired so she would go home so I could watch porn and masturbate. The feeling and rush it gave me was awesome! My girlfriend despised porn and thought it was for perverts. I would have never suggested her watching it with me as it was my world all the same. She would have wrecked the experience for me if she watched it with me.

I did this secretly for the entire time I was with her. I am sure she suspected it as she saw links to porn sites on my computer as well. There were a couple of times she brought her suspicions up but I quickly denied it and it turned into a fight and this would put me on the outs with her for days.

In terms of masturbation, I was up to doing it anywhere from 7-10 times a day. It was a ritual for me. I used the same side of the bed all of the time. I had a selection of lubricants and oils, non-sexual in nature as not to raise suspicion. I used tissue paper to clean up and always flushed the "evidence" down the toilet. I found that if I saw a really good looking girl in a public place whether I was alone or with my girlfriend, I would commit what she looked like to memory and use it later when I was alone.

I realized I had an addiction to masturbation when I would literally get anxious, irritable and very angry if I couldn't do it for periods of time or when I most wanted to do it. There were some times I wanted to "get off" so bad, but couldn't because my girlfriend was there. Here I have a girlfriend, but I wanted to do it for myself, on the fantasy I created.

I will say this much... There is not a woman out there who can compete or measure up to the fantasy. It could even be the model or woman you get to have that you are fantasizing over, and even she can't live up to the fantasy or expectation.

Ironically, while we were still together I once let her try to masturbate me. It was not good at all and it completely turned me off. A woman doesn't stand a chance when a guy is this dedicated to satisfying himself!

When applying *Object Relations Theory* to the Madonna complex, you get another Freudian/Psychoanalytical concept known as transference. In transference individuals act and react toward someone who reminds them of someone else, usually their mother or father. Is it any wonder men from dysfunctional mother-son relationships seek out women who remind them of their mothers and then eventually treat them like their mothers?

When you examine transference and the Madonna complex, the reason men choose not to have sex with their wives is because their wives remind them too much of their mothers -- having sex with their wives would be like having sex with their mothers. It's not that these men find their wives unattractive because they don't! Instead, they are just not "sexually/physically" into them because their wives are more like a mother figure. In fact, these "mother" figures possess a sacred resemblance for some!

Interestingly, transference prevents a man from having sex with his wife, for one of these two reasons:

1) His wife reminds him too much of his mother, whom he reveres, holds sacred and views her with untarnished purity.

2) His wife reminds him of his mother who hurt, neglected or mistreated him as a child and he despises her.

In either scenario, his wife vicariously becomes the physical re-incarnate of his mother. There is not a snowball chance in hell of her receiving the physical attention she yearns for.

In the first line of reason, she is figuratively the "Madonna"-- pure, wholesome, sacred... A saint!

Having sexual relations with her outside of the purpose of procreation is perceived as dirty by her husband. In fact, even the act of making children with her is perceived as tainted. The thought of any other kind of sex; prolonged kissing, foreplay, petting, oral sex and especially anal sex, are abominations and are wrong! There is a wonderful scene in the movie *Analyze This* starring Billy Crystal and Robert DeNiro where Crystal, who plays a shrink, Dr. Ben Sobel, helps Mafia leader DeNiro deal with aspects of his past. Crystal finds DeNiro having sex with a call girl and asks DeNiro's character Paul Vitti "Why?". Vitti promptly responds by asserting that he is not going to put his "thing" in the mouth of his children's mother because it's just wrong! Interestingly, the idea of infidelity being wrong is not even raised by Vitti. Sure this is just a movie, but when men possess this type of Madonna complex transference issue, they really believe they are doing the noble thing by "cheating" on their wives and having a paid professional, or mistress engage in the sexual acts they would never subjugate their wives too.

Furthermore, some would be just too embarrassed to ask for, or engage their wives in certain sexual acts. By having sex with another woman, they don't "compromise" their perceived integrities or their wife's. As twisted as it sounds, this is what they truly believe!

In the second line of reasoning, they married a psychological or even physical carbon of their mother. Interestingly, some of these men will even marry or date a woman much more older than them, in order to accomplish their Madonna complex goal. They truly go all the way in recapitulating the circumstances surrounding their mother. The one constant they hold onto is the bitterness, loathing and hatred they project toward their mothers whom their wives now serve as surrogates for.

Most men who select wives who remind them of the mothers, eventually end up despising their wives because they remind them too much of their moms. In many cases they are not even physically attracted to them. Instead, the women serve more as companions or comfort figures -- mothers, sisters or nurturers who make the men feel secure in the relationship. The wives are most likely the ones to cook the men's meals, wash their clothes and oversee the house. If they have kids together, then caring for them and raising them is the wives' primary job. Since many of these men prefer older women, or women who do not want kids, the maternal figure role holds closer to form. If they do have kids, then it is no surprise the men vie and might even compete for the maternal attention and affection their own kids are getting from their wives.

When a couple like this, does have sex, the man either performs for the purpose of procreation, or to save the marriage/relationship. In the first situation, a part of him may feel the need to sew his seed and keep his gene pool going. The act of sex serves as nothing more as a means to an end -- getting her pregnant. In fact, getting her pregnant and keeping her busy with children is one way for him to "get out of having sex with her". He encourages her to put the children first so she is too tired to have sex with him.

Conversely, when he gets involved with a much older woman, he may choose one that is needy for affection and is more than happy to "just have" a younger man in her life. Even though he neglects and rejects her, she would rather be with someone, namely him for all of the wrong reasons than be alone for all of the right reasons. In some cases when his wife "needs" physical contact -- sexual relations with him, he usually only fulfills her needs to save their relationship. She may threaten to leave him, or he might feel that she will cheat on him, so he reacts sporadically to appease her. Just like Al Bundy did, on the long running television series *Married With Children*, where he would occasionally have sex with his wife Peggy to shut her up -- and he would do his manly, husbandly duties as often as one would be getting their air ducts in their homes cleaned out. Sure this television show was a sitcom and made fun of this situation, however in real life it is all true, and some wives literally have to beg their husbands for sex!

Even though she is sex-starved, he usually is not! Either he is arousing and satisfying himself through masturbation, or he is having sexual relations with a mistress or sex trade worker who he finds more attractive. Have you ever heard the sarcastic expression some men brag, "I got married so I could then go out and look for a girlfriend!" This is not too far a stretch from reality! Some men do get married so they will have someone who will care for them and be a mother figure. By marrying their "mother-like wife", this frees them up literally to go out and exercise their machismo freedoms to be men...

Some men feel the need to go out and cheat because this demonstrates their potency and freedom. Moreover, this is their means for celebrating being a "man" and the traditional freedoms of being a man!

In Chapter Four we will discuss these rationalizations in greater depth and the precarious reasons which deal with the "Why?".

CHAPTER SUMMARY -- KEY POINTS

1) According to founding psychology theorists such as Sigmund Freud, attitudes as well as gender/sexual identities start in childhood. Who and what we become early on, makes us into what we are as adults.

2) From the beginning of time there have always existed an uneven playing field between the sexes. Men have always enjoyed the greater amount of power in the real world and in the bedroom.

3) Men often times seek out women who remind them of their mothers. Furthermore, they are likely to treat their wives/girlfriends the same way their fathers treated their mothers.

4) In the Madonna complex, men possessing ideals with regards to the complex, view sex as a means only to procreation.

5) Some men equate sex with ownership and conquering. The more sex they have with different women, the perception of power within themselves becomes greater.

CHAPTER TWO

HISTORICAL ORIGINS OF THE MADONNA COMPLEX

The common thread that binds nearly all animal species seems to be that males are willing to abandon all sense and decorum, even to risk their lives, in the frantic quest for sex.

Randy Thornhill and Craig T. Palmer, *A Natural History of Rape*

In the last chapter we examined the origins of the Madonna/Madonna-whore complex based on the theories and work of famous Psychoanalyst Sigmund Freud. Like the formation of any theory, the Madonna complex has its historical origins created and perpetuated by society and the culture of that time period. In this chapter, we will delve into some of the cultural contexts and threads for where the Madonna complex really sprung to life and picked up momentum.

Much of the historical contexts which are tied and bind around the Madonna complex can be traced back to both European and Latin American roots. Marianismo is a term often linked to the Madonna complex. The concept is derived from the Roman Catholic belief that the Virgin Mother Mary was both a virgin and the lady Madonna. The theme surrounding Marianismo is moral virtue which places women on a somewhat semi-divine level. When discussing women in the context of Marianismo, they are represented as being morally superior to men. The purity that woman are said to possess makes them spiritually stronger. Some might assert perhaps this is the reason men are more driven by the "physical" versus the intimate, "spiritual" nature of their being. Could this be the reason why men have a more difficult time remaining faithful to their mates?

When comparing the genders, women are the ones believed to possess greater moral strength and "purity" than their male counterparts. Today women are still perceived the ones purer at heart, spirit and sanctity. Don't believe it? What is the traditional color women are still expected to wear to their weddings? White was and is the color of purity -- being a virgin! Does this mean that all the brides wearing white to their weddings are still virgins? That would make for one heck of an interesting survey!

One of the qualities of Marianismo also includes the notion that women are the physically weaker, gentle, docile and passive gender. Women are "softer" in both their physicality and in their personalities. This makes them more passive than men. As a result of this, men are the aggressors when it comes to sex and procreation. Even though most women long to have children, men tend to be the aggressors who, "hunt", "stalk", "chase" and pursue their mates. Even though things have greatly changed in today's society -- women are now more assertive, aggressive and dominant when it comes to selecting and pursuing mates, in many parts of the world, even in North America, the virtue of women still being the weaker more passive of the two in terms of relationships is very much alive, well and the norm!

A large part of the Marianismo process in terms of dating/courting involves "the game". Traditionally, women prefer or necessitate being "chased" by men to preserve their pure virtues -- they don't come off appearing as some kind of wild, loose cannons. On the other hand, some men prefer and even like the chase. What man doesn't like a challenge? By their very nature, men are more competitive than women. Within male circles, "conquering a woman" either sexually or attaining a relationship proves a man's "manhood"! For some men, the idea of "conquering and taking no prisoners" -- having sex with as many women as possible and then moving onto the next, has been ingrained at an early age for men. Is it any wonder some types of men are referred to as "Don Juan" or "Casanova"?

Even though women are taught not to give in too quickly while men are pursuing them for relationships and/or sexual relations, inevitably she will give in if she wants to have a marriage and a family. Interestingly, the harder some women play in terms of surrendering themselves, some men welcome and adorn the challenge. In fact, some men are all about the game/challenge only and once they get their prey, they drop them like bad habits.

Within the domain of dominance, when it comes to sexual relations there does exist a hypocrisy/conflict regarding sexual purity. Some men desire virgins only to be their wives. Moreover, some men prefer virgins only to have sex with even though they themselves have been ridden like a quarter-ride at a carnival!

Conversely there are certain men who will only have sex with non-virgins. Something within them makes them believe that deflowering a virgin and robbing her of this virtue is a carnal sin. Perhaps as many men have evolved in terms of spiritual purity in today's generation, just as many women have evolved in terms of their sexual liberation.

Marianismo holds the greater virtue of life -- women are the maternal caregivers who give life. They bring babies into the world. They keep life going as we know it!

There is also a tremendous connection between women and babies. Babies are seen as the weakest, softest, docile, dependent creatures on the face of this earth. Who brings this very delicate creature into the world and then nurtures it? If you answered women then you got it! Since women are capable of bringing something so beautiful and delicate into the world then they too must possess these same attributes. Therefore to sexually harm or rob a woman who is a mother, or potential mother of her "virtue" would be like harming her babies directly/indirectly.

The Virgin Mother was the one who gave birth to Jesus. For this she was given the supreme title as Mother of God! If Mary is the Mother of God, then she is revered with tremendous admiration and veneration. She becomes symbolic and representative of all mothers, even women for that matter. If that becomes the perception of women in general, then she should possess the same pure qualities as the Virgin Mother. Furthermore, it would be expected that men would honour her with tremendous respect for the qualities of "immaculate purity" she possesses!

Mothers are considered the ultimate fibres in society which create, sustain and maintain life. Motherhood is a dignified, most honourable full-time job for many mothers. Since she is all of the aforementioned, then she is held in greater esteem and placed in a higher status in most societies. She is to be honoured, respected and appreciated for the good that she does for mankind!

When you combine all facets of the Marianismo concept together, men who buy into it and their wives who accept it, the following is what can be expected in marriages/relationships:

1) He is expected to respect and maintain the sanctity of his wife's purity.

2) He is expected to view his wife as a passive individual and she is expected to remain passive -- physically, sexually and in major decision making.

3) He is expected to abstain from all sexual activities with his wife unless it is for the purpose of procreation.

4) She is expected to nurture his children and remain spiritually pure to set an example for the children.

5) If he feels the needs to "have sex", then outside affairs are in order to preserve his wife's purity, his wholesome intentions for her while at the same time satisfying his sexual cravings and massaging his male ego.

MY PRIM AND PROPER QUEEN - A CASE STUDY

I was married a few years back to a woman I loved very much. I waited until my thirties to marry. She was in her late 20's. She was still living at home with her parents when we met and until we got married.

From the get-go there were both implied and explicit rules. She would live at home until her father okayed her potential husband. Needless to say it took a lot of work on my part to prove I was worthy of her and could live up to what was expected of me.

She had never been "with a man" in the sexual sense until we married. She talked about it and how fun it would be before we were married, but once we did get married, nothing really changed. I don't think that she was frigid by choice. It was part of her mindset. For whatever reason "not having sex" was ingrained into her thinking. She was taught it was a "duty" a wife does for her man, whether she wanted to or not. It made me feel like I was always taking something from her I shouldn't be. It got to the point where I didn't even want to anymore, since it made me feel guilty.

It was when we discussed having children that the idea of sex appealed to her most. Once again it parlayed into nothing more than a "duty" to fulfill -- give her husband kids, give her parents grandchildren and of course, be a mother. I knew that once the child creation duties were done, I would probably never again appeal to her as a man. There probably would no longer be sexual relations.

I started to look elsewhere and wanted to actively engage in an affair. I came close! I kissed and made out with a woman and stopped it there. That was really hard to do! I wanted to do more, but didn't want to be a cheat.

I decided against having children with my wife. This upset her as well as her parents. I just didn't want to have kids with her. I think I also created this manoeuvre as a power play to get out of the marriage. It worked!

We started to drift apart further than we already were and eventually this strained relations between her parents and me. This put even greater negative pressure on our marriage. It got to the point where she eventually left me and moved back home with her parents. Within the next few months, she filed for divorce, which I accepted as I took a job promotion in another city.

It's funny how you think things will change or you can change someone to grow into fitting with you. I used to think that I was living with her parents too whenever she spoke. Ironically I was! We carry around with us what our parents teach us and in some ways we become them!

Misogyny is another antecedent to the rise of the Madonna complex. Misogyny is a loathing and hatred for women by men and even other women, just because they are female. If you travel back to ancient times, you can see the rise of this hateful perception of women. It was then that women were treated as second class citizens -- not as valuable or revered as men. In fact, the famous philosopher Aristotle once postulated that women themselves are nothing more than non-perfect men! Men were created to be the superior and the perfect gender while women were created with many impurities and deformities which made them only half of what men were. Throughout centuries, thinking and rationale as such has placed and kept women in subordinate positions and put men in the position of referent power holders. Men traditionally have had the power to hold the key positions in society and make most if not all of the major decisions. Even though this sexist, conceptual thinking originated in Europe and Asia and eventually Africa, it has traveled across the Atlantic Ocean and has existed since the USA was colonized and eventually became an independent country. Sexism and the sexual exploitation of women is still around in parts of the USA! Just for the sake of interest...When was the last time the USA had a female president? Interestingly, the USA elected a Black American president before they elected a woman president. Not too long ago, Black Americans were slaves and even after the abolishment of slavery, they were for many decades treated as second class citizens, even after the 1970's and Women's Liberation. Yet, a Black American man made it to the position of Commander and Chief before a woman. Does this mean anything? Should it matter? If you ask some women or Neo-feminist groups they would respond by saying, "Heck yeah!".

Misogyny in its purest form depicts an extreme animosity, even hatred against women. When was the last time you heard a "dumb blonde" joke or some other sexist-laden, chauvinistic joke about a women, or thrown in the direction of a woman? Much like the example of the Black American President, people are usually quicker to the punch to get bent out of shape when jokes are laced with racism or religiosity, than they are when it involves putting down a woman. Why is that? Moreover, misogyny is not just a disdain against women by men, as some women are just as guilty. Have you ever watched magazine-type television shows that track celebrities, entertainers and models? In many cases, women are more critical than men!

Misogyny is perpetuated in many different facets in today's society. With the advent of multi-media and "other" new forms of entertainment, you can find it rampant still in television shows, movies, books, commercials, and especially pornography. Is it any wonder violence against women still occurs at such a high rate? Ads and women's magazines might have some women convinced that they have "Come a long way baby!" , but it is nothing more than an illusion. Worst of all, much of what demeans and places women in perverse situations is perpetuated by women themselves! Men for the most part in the western world have had to become more accountable when they "exploit" or demean women. Have you ever heard of "zero tolerance" or sexual harassment in the workplace? In some countries and states men get legally hammered if they demean a woman. Conversely, women can say what they want against other women, whether it be sexist or degrading, they are not called chauvinists and usually do not have to answer to these charges.

Many women's magazines portray women, or send out the message that "women are just not good enough" in terms of their bodies, looks and sexiness. Think about it for a moment...Who publishes these women's magazines and who usually buys them? It's not men! Furthermore, who stars as the models in these magazines, often times appearing too thin and looking malnourished? If you said women, then once again you are correct. Is it any wonder so many women suffer from eating disorders such as; anorexia nervosa, bulimia and compulsive eating? Is it any wonder women are the number one clients of plastic surgery -- breast implants, liposuction, Botox, facelifts, etc.? Sure men like to look at beautiful, sexy women, but whatever happened to sexual equality and women's liberation? Why should a woman's imperfect tummy require her to have a tummy tuck but a man's beer gut make him cool because he can drink other guys under the table? Also, men love pornography! Did you know there are over 100 million web pages devoted to porn on the Internet making it more popular than sports? Sure men might be considered "pigs" for watching and buying porn but... Who is choosing to star in these movies and make a decent living out of it? We think you know the answer to that question!

At the end of the day, the negative message still exists for women: It is okay to feel disdain and self-contempt for yourself and your body! Why is it that women have to be the "hated" gender according to misogyny? When affirmative action and women's liberation started to spring to life, in many parts of the world the "man" was viewed as the bad guy. The dark force from the evil empire. But even this negative perception of men did not last long. Even though women had been oppressed for centuries by men, as soon as men were asked and sometimes forced to let women become equal, or even "have their powerful jobs", this threw things out of whack and made men the "victims". Although it was "just" a few years, or perhaps a decade, this was however not allowed to last because men were being victimized and two wrongs did not make a right! Hence, everything in the dynamics of the work world changed and people were firmly hired for the experience and qualifications they brought to the table.

What is the major impact of misogyny on the Madonna complex? When you look at the Madonna complex in this light then the answer is simple: Objects! if you wish to dissect the term "object" as related to women, then the qualifier which often times first pops up to describe them is "sex"... SEX OBJECTS!

If a man believes the work-world has become exceedingly difficult to conquer (first competing with other men and now women), what is the best way to "objectify" his competition? He can conquer her, possess her, own her! He can do this with sex! Could this be the reason he loves her and leaves her? She became his conquest... Literally; been there, done that and used her. In the male world there is the concept of "up-manship", the ability to be or feel superior over another man. A guy does a favour for his buddy and he knows he has the upper hand on his friend -- his buddy owes him. In misogyny, the man who uses a woman sexually, believes that he "owns" her, even if it is just for one night.

The interesting part of misogyny viewed from this frame of reference is that it really isn't about the sex, but rather that particular woman to have sex with him. The fulfillment of this experience for him is magnified if it was a woman who initially rejected him or played immensely hard to get. At the end of the day he "got her" and used her to fulfill his own means to an end. Woman who get used for this method of madness are used as sex objects --TROPHIES!

There is the old saying that the apple doesn't fall too far from the tree. If he observed his father treating first his mother and then other women like this, or his single mother was treated like this repeatedly by other men, then he is most likely to collect the torch and run with it! This is how he is most likely to treat women in the future. Or he might already be doing it.

Without delving into the whole battered woman's syndrome/cycle of abuse, misogyny perhaps contributes to the cycle of abuse, for many of the aforementioned reasons we developed. The only thing which truly separates battered woman syndrome from the Madonna complex, is the sexual relation component. Men may beat their wives/girlfriends because they witnessed attributes of misogyny as children, however some are really "in love" with their mates and enjoy/choose to have sex with them only. They perceive them neither as overly pure/wholesome, nor do they view them as bitches or sluts.

Whether men choose to perceive women from the perspective of Marianismo or misogyny, either way women never possess the equality they have longed and strived for. If they are hoisted high on a pedestal they are sanctified as too good for sexual relations. If they are degraded to the depths of a gutter then they are not good enough for love. Either way the Madonna complex places women in a -- damned if they do or damned if they don't -- position, while both genders are the culprits of perpetuating and keeping this irrational thought process flourishing in the 21st Century.

In the chapters to follow you will learn how the Madonna complex has led to and continues to be the cause and demise of marriages, relationships, families and even one's own personality. Even though we have evolved in terms of technological advancement, the same cannot be said to be true in our attitudes toward sex. There will always be the nay-sayers who will claim that it is just a phase or cycle that humans go through.

Well, this cycle has been around one heck of a long time... Say, centuries! The advancement of technology has definitely aided and abetted individuals to embark on extramarital affairs, infidelity and create/feed their sex addictions.

CHAPTER SUMMARY - KEY POINTS

1) Marianismo is a term often linked to the Madonna complex. The theme surrounding Marianismo is moral virtue which places women on a somewhat semi-divine level.

2) Marianismo depicts women as the physically weaker, gentle, docile and passive gender. Women are "softer" in both their physicality and personality.

3) Misogyny is another aspect of the Madonna complex. Misogyny is a loathing and hatred for women by men and even other women just because they are female.

4) Misogyny in its purest form depicts an extreme animosity, even hatred against women.

5) The same negative attitudes about sex and women are still around today.

CHAPTER THREE

GENDER

DIFFERENCES

Insanity: doing the same thing over and over again and expecting different results.

Albert Einstein

So far we have had some discussion on what the Madonna complex is, and where it comes from. The Madonna complex is interesting because we witness the issues mostly in males. Whether or not something similar exists in females is still up for debate and don't worry we will definitely get into that a bit later! But just to give you a bit of a preview: While it is true that Freud had a very controversial theory as stated in the previous chapters, later the Neo-Freudians came along and stated that young females went through an analogous complex to the Oedipus. The Electra complex was revolutionary in the sense that young females were said to have this unconscious sexual desire for their fathers which eventually turned into learning about the concept of femininity through their mothers and the special relationship with their fathers.

The reason the Electra complex was so revolutionary during the early (as well as prior to and after) the mid twentieth century, was because females were supposed to remain limited in their sexual experiences because of social conventions of gender. Much of the research at the time was done on males due to females being second class citizens and at times referred to as "degenerates." Therefore the concept of the Madonna complex traditionally directed at males, could not have held a place in the domain of female psychology and behaviour because of the time period. Apparently, according to the theory, this is all because of females lacking a penis and unconsciously blaming their mothers for their misfortunes. What Freud's theory contended was that back in the day, Freud's time and prior, daughters secretly wished their fathers would impregnate them so that they could bare his children. When daughters realized that their fathers were ultimately tied to their mothers, they revoked their animosity toward their mothers because they finally realized they did not want to lose their mother's love. If they couldn't possess their father's then why not get close to the woman who possesses the man they want most, so they too can learn how to one day possess a man like dear old dad!

It is interesting to examine these two concepts because in our current world of behaviour and psychology we still see the many strong indications of the Oedipus and Electra complex in the simple saying "Daddy's little girl" and "Mommy's little boy." For example, some little boys constantly cling to their mothers and will not let them out of their site. There exists a certain level of intimacy that little boys are trying to get met. When you think about it, this is a male's first real degree of intimacy with a woman... His mother. Interestingly, most research has shown that the mother-child bond is the tightest bond between all humans. Children who are/feel rejected by their mothers are more likely to develop difficulties in creating secure relationships later in life. This is especially true for boys as mothers who reject them or push them away will most likely seek out women with cold, aloof and rejecting personalities. Those who feel loved and accepted by their mothers will seek out women who are loving and create secure, positive emotional environments.

The same holds true for little girls. For example, little girls who sit by her father's side staring at him while he is working on the car is waiting for his attention and approval -- an intimate connection with her! Later in life if that little girl was rejected or neglected by her father, she is most likely to seek out psychological carbon copies of her father -- abuse, neglectful and disrespectful men. Conversely, when her father demonstrates love and acceptance, thus valuing her company, she is most likely to seek out that kind of man. In essence, the Law of Attraction starts very early on in life in terms of the selection of future mates!

Studies and discussions surrounding females and sexuality are much more laid back. Women can and do enjoy a hefty appetite for sex as men do, but they seek out a more emotional/intimate type of connection as well. Much more research is being done on female sexuality these days. What has come to the forefront of research involving women and sexuality is the question of women who are in monogamous relationships. What happens when their spouse does not want to have sex with them? How do they react? What has been found is rather than brood over sexual rejection from their own spouse (which is of course common at the onset of the sexless situation), rejected women tend to fantasize more and get turned on by other men they are not in a relationship with. In fact, it is more common today for women to get turned on after they have been in a monogamous/sexually exclusive relationship for several years by having thoughts of other men.

Still, the Madonna complex raises many questions, most of which we stated in our introduction. However, the question still remains on whether or not this could be something that is "normal", in terms of the "normal" limit of human sexual behaviour. Or if it is rather a severe mental health issue as discussed more openly in main stream media and demonstrated in movies like Psycho. Keep in mind we are not asserting most or all men look, act and talk like Norman Bates..." Mother!" They also do not go onto becoming serial killers. Rather some become serial gigolos!

Gender differences exist in all aspects of society and in most cultures. Right or wrong, they are alive and continue to come to a medium ground or get worse in separating genders further. It is believed that once males and females are on the same sexual "playing field" only then will gender differences start to subside. What is meant by that is that only when most women have sex as their male counterparts, without the guilt, shame, and anxiety around their behaviour, then only will women be equal to men in terms of gender differences and sex. Yes... It really is all about sex!

Traditionally, males have been and still are, emotionally ardent. They have never really been encouraged or, for that matter, been provided with the tools to express emotion. The expression of emotion is at the core of true intimacy -- it is all about feeling! Many people, especially men confuse intimacy with feeling. This is where men get led down the garden path to getting things wrong when it comes to intimacy. Intimacy is about feeling and expression emotion. And let's face it... You can't feel unless you think! When women complain they are not getting enough "intimacy" in their relationships, they are referring to the "thinking" kind. They want to know what is on their man's mind. Many women have claimed to find the sexiest part of a man to be his mind. It is the "mind" that makes the personality which most women are attracted to! If a guy truly wanted to "score" sexually with a woman, he would have a better chance exposing his mind -- feelings, rather than talking about his endowment. By the way, I.Q. is always much higher than endowment size so perhaps a triple digit number might be more appealing than a single digit number, especially when the number is in the bottom half of ten!

Most males who possess the Madonna complex have searched for intimacy with their own mothers but have faced rejection. Their mothers are usually cold women who may or may not take care of them physically, but the lack of emotions is a constant... They are not present! They may have been reprimanded and disciplined by their mothers, but felt unwanted, misunderstood or unappreciated where it mattered most -- the feeling department. The ramifications of this lack of maternal intimacy is damaging down the road! Boys often times grow up with this unconscious duality within them desiring intimacy while forced to accept the societal demands of masculinity. In the end, the macho component in them wins over the soft, emotional persona. This leads them to becoming anything less than androgynous (the ability to identify, accept and empathize with masculine and feminine attributes) as they do their best to fight off the urges for intimacy. Have you ever seen what happens when a woman asks her man to sit down because she "needs to talk"? You'd swear some men perceive this intimate talking as her requesting him to have a sex change operation. Interestingly, there are some men who equate the two... One being an emotional sex change (talking) and one being a real physical sex change!

TOM'S BOUT WITH THE MADONA COMPLEX –

A CASE STUDY

It was suggested to Tom at age 27 that he might have something called the Madonna complex. He remembers his mother not being there for him growing up but does remember always having clean clothes and food on the table. Both his parents were somewhat distant but he states that his mother was much more cold. He does not remember getting a hug from his mother and does not remember seeing his mother and father show affection towards one another.

Tom was not married at 27 but did have a girlfriend of three years. Tom stopped wanting to have sex with her after the first year. Their sex life dwindled to what became twice a year. Tom's girlfriend always wanted to "talk" about where their relationship was headed long-term. He didn't want to address this topic! However, Tom had desire for other women and had numerous affairs outside of his relationship.

Eventually the cheating caught up to Tom. The relationship ended miserably for him and he had a succession of other relationships that ended badly. He struggled when it came to forming relationships with women. The easiest part for Tom was having sex with women as he didn't have to communicate. He remembers that in the beginning of starting any relationship, he would try to have sexual intimacy as soon as possible with a woman to get her to like him and connect with him. After having sex with him a few times, he knew they were emotionally vulnerable to him. He knew he could then worry about less when it came to discussing the emotional components of the relationship. When these women asked Tom to dig down and share emotions with them, this is when he felt they were trying to control him and force him into being something he wasn't. The only way he felt he could regain control over his life, and feel free, was to seek out another woman and have sex with her. He found this liberating!

The only problem with this series of events was that the cheating would cause him to lose his relationship, but he would cling to the mistress he was having "just sex" with. He would then feel compelled to be in a relationship because he did not want to be alone as that would mean he was rejected. Herein lied the greatest problem! The mistress who would then become his lover/partner would then place the "unrealistic demands" on him to express himself emotionally with her. For Tom this meant bailing and finding another sex partner.

What Tom didn't realize was he was master and commander of this chain of repeated failed relationships. Most of his problems as an adult stemmed from the lack of personal intimacy he had with his mother. He truly believed the best and only way to keep a woman interested in him was through sex. For him, he knew that if he had to open up emotionally, he knew women would see through him which meant seeing a disdain for his own mother. After several counselling sessions, Tom realized his self-destructive behaviour. Furthermore, he realized he also loathed women and was projecting the feelings he had toward his mother on the women he got involved with.

Tom decided not to date women until he felt better about himself and could learn to appreciate and love himself. He realized that he could only express love and give it, when he could learn to feel it inside him. Tom was also encouraged to write letters to his mother expressing the hurt and disappointment he felt toward her. These letters were never sent, rather they served as a cathartic exercise which allowed him to release the negative feelings he had, which punished him from within.

Insanity: doing the same thing over and over again and expecting different results! We chose Albert Einstein's famous quote at the beginning of this chapter as we thought it best explains why so many people have repeatedly failed relationships. Many point the finger at the quality of people they meet and date blaming them for the repeated failures. When in fact, they should start looking within, because only then will they see they are their own worst enemy!

In our discussion on gender differences in intimacy, the expectations of girls is the opposite -- they are taught emotions and intimacy. They are taught to openly discuss their feelings. This is one of the reasons females are remarkably better at intimacy than their male counterparts. Even when a female is raised in a family where there was an aloof or distant cold mother or father involved, they still become better at intimacy. With females, there is often times not the duality of societal direction dictating how a woman is to behave with regard to her emotion. On the other hand, the expectation surrounding her sexual behaviour is an altogether different story!

A boy's mother becomes thought of as the "sacred" person who keeps him alive-- nourishing him and caring for him. He loves and values his mother for this. However, as an adult man getting involved with a girlfriend, once the courting phase is over he unconsciously places his girlfriend on a similar level of expectation to his mother. The girlfriend often times plays right into this by wanting to take care of him, feed him, wash his clothes, etc.

A conflict of interest exists within the mind of the man who perceives his mother and girlfriend for being reasonable copies for one another -- the Madonna complex. There can be a tremendous amount of guilt in the mind of the man who possesses the Madonna complex. Often times the girlfriend or the wife is seen through the same lens as the mother. This is not good! He does not want to find his "mother" in the woman he chose to get involved with. When he does see dear old mom in her, all bets are off! He dare not view her as sexy or attractive. For this man, love and sex do not go together -- they can't exist in the same realm. This may unconsciously be correlated with incest taboos. By having sex with his girlfriend/wife would equate with a non-abusive incestuous relationship because in his mind, his girlfriend/wife is his mother. So instead, sex is reserved for what is perceived as the "dirty" woman, as a way to ward off any feelings of love.

JACK'S STORY - A CASE STUDY

Jack is a 42 year old male who has been married for five years. Jack loves his wife very much but states he has no sexual attraction for her even though he can admit that he finds her to be a "pretty" woman. They have sex roughly two to three times a year and Jack has to fantasize about other women while having sex with his wife. Jack's wife describes herself as a very sexual person and enjoys giving oral sex as well as initiating sex with Jack. Jack turns his wife down on a consistent basis. At this point his wife states she is about to have an affair because of the rejection from her husband. Jack does not understand why he feels this way about his wife. Jack does have a history of an overbearing mother who he states he admires but is not a very connected woman. He remembers no times where his mother was affectionate towards him.

Whenever Jack's wife makes any negative or derogatory comments about his mother, he loses his cool. Jack often times makes undesirable comments about his mother. Only he is allowed to make these comments. His wife is not even allowed to agree with them or jack gets upset with her. Jack's wife notices that Jack reveres his mother, almost out of fear and intimidation. She wants to have an affair not only to feel physically wanted by a man, but also to compare another man's mindset with Jack's. Jack's wife blames Jack's mother but also believes she must possess flaws too if Jack continually rejects her.

Jack's wife knows the guilt will eat her up if she chooses to cheat on Jack. With that said, she opts to see a counsellor privately and discuss the situation with the counsellor to gain some insights. She selects a male counsellor hoping he might be able to relate to Jack and Jack's upbringing.

To date her extramarital fling has been put on hold. She hopes it never comes to fruition! After a couple of months she discusses her therapy with Jack. Seeing how his marriage is in potential trouble, Jack begins seeing a therapist. For the first time in his life, he gets insight into his own life.

There is no doubt that Jack possesses a form of the Madonna complex. Over the next couple of months of intensive therapy and education, he learned how much he put his wife in the position of being a representation of power his mother and how he lost sexual attraction for her. The two of them did not want to have children so sex could not be about procreation which is also seen often in relationships where the male has the Madonna complex -- he only has sex for the purpose of procreation!

Since we are exploring gender differences in this chapter it is important to look briefly at a female who has a similar type of issue. In general, we know that the

Madonna complex is thought to be a man's issue but it is apparent that women engage in compartmentalizing things too! Women do it in two ways:

1) Women are very aware of the roles they are in, as well as what they should be striving for. Women will often feel forced to identify with either the Madonna or the whore aspect. This poses a fundamental problem for women in that it creates a juxtaposition for them. They are caught on an either/or polarity. They figuratively can't have their cake and eat it too! Women are told to be "Madonna-like" but if they are not "sexually loose" too, then they are prudes and equally not as wanted by their male counterparts.

In essence, if they behave too virtuous, then men won't want them because they are boring. On the other hand, if they behave sexually, they might get rejected because they are floozies! In their minds, if they behave too virtuous, they will only attract "boring" non-sexual men and then get stuck in sexless marriages. Conversely, if they behave sexually, they are more likely to attract the "bad boy" who is all about sex and may not treat them like ladies. Damned if she does and damned if she doesn't! Interestingly, when she possesses both qualities "virtuous" and "sexy", once she does naughty things, it seems the virtuous things are more likely to get forgotten and she gets a name for herself. How many times have you read about a "good girl" who does one bad thing or gets involved in a scandal only to have her name ripped through the tabloids like a cheap hooker? When a "good" man gets caught in this same type of scandal, things are chalked up to "bad judgement", a "simple mistake", or "men just being men". Perhaps you might remember a certain U.S. President who "just did oral sex". How quickly was he pardoned and allowed to regain his dignity? Why do men get a mulligan and women don't?

2) Women who grow up with an unemotional father who denies them of emotional bonding, often times develop issues with sex and love. As we stated in this book, children are products of their parents. How parents demonstrate love in front of their children, as well as how they communicate with their kids, goes a long way in helping them form their own secure relationships as adults.

Women who select absent/distant emotional mates were most likely to have fathers who taught them that this is how men act. They are most likely to become one of the two sexual personalities for their man; cold or overbearing.

And if the woman was raised in a frigid type of family and witnessed her mother being affectionately cold to her father and him being cold in turn to her, that is how she is most likely to act. She will probably select a man who dislikes sex. If he does like sex, she will rarely engage in it and then when she does, he has to do all of the work and she doesn't enjoy it.

On the other hand, if her father rejected her mother and she saw her mother trying to salvage the marriage, she will do likewise. She will select men who have difficulty committing or staying in a relationship. Furthermore, she may feel the need to sacrifice herself physically, emotionally, and even financially to get him to love her and stay.

To close out this chapter we chose to use Melissa's case study to demonstrate how the Madonna complex can be viewed/used from a female's perspective.

MELISSA'S HYPOCRISY OF THE MADONNA COMPLEX - A CASE STUDY

Melissa is a young attractive Caucasian female. Melissa was a very interesting individual to interview because her perspective on the Madonna complex was right on... That is if you traditionally heard it from a man's mouth. In this case, Melissa sort of tilted the tables in the other direction. Here were her the exact words which reflect the essence of the Madonna complex, " I don't see how love and sex are even remotely connected. How can someone love someone they have sex with?"

According to Melissa, she could only keep a boyfriend for about two months, complaining she never had orgasms. Melissa grew frustrated and tired of having neither; love and fulfilling sexual relations. You see Melissa was unable to connect sex and love together and therefore was not able to give herself fully away to a male partner. This prevented her from committing to long term relationships as well as receiving the pleasure of orgasms. She felt like she was caught between a rock and a hard place. In the beginning she used to blame men, especially those she dated and had sex with. It was their fault for not bringing her to climax. She grew to despise men! In fact, she began to separate the two, sex and love. If she couldn't "get off" with the man she was with, how could she love him, especially when she despised him for not satisfying her? Sure she was always able to satisfy them, but this totally felt unfair to her! She found that the only men she could "love" in a companionate way were "just friends". There was no pressure for them to get her satisfied so they were safe targets because there was no sex.

Melissa claimed she became so frustrated with men and their sexual performance that she started to vicariously live through them when they would climax because of her. She started to enjoy the rush of getting a guy off. Moreover, she visualized in her mind that the orgasm her mates were having really belong to her. She was the one having them. Fantasies can only go so far, especially when you are having sexual relations with a real human being. This process led her toward additional frustration. Eventually she caved in!

Melissa eventually sought the aid of a counsellor after reading an ad in a women's magazine involving sex and frigidity. After some intense counselling and soul searching, the therapist led Melissa to the deep realization that she was "holding out" emotionally with men. To have an orgasm at the hands of a man meant that he had "control over her", at least that was Melissa's perception.

When the therapist discussed Melissa's childhood, it was found that her father was an alcoholic who had regular affairs on her mother. Her mother eventually left him. She witnessed the psychological hurt in her mother and vowed she would never let that happen to her. Her promise rang true. The reason she couldn't have an orgasm is because she wouldn't surrender her trust to a man. All men became representations of her father. He treated women as sex objects and ironically didn't have sex with his own wife, Melissa's mother. For Melissa, abstinence even while having sexual relations was her safe guard.

After months of therapy and at the suggestion of the therapist, Melissa was encouraged to have "just male" friends and no casual sex. She was asked to establish within herself permission to trust herself first (her decisions) as well as men. Once she could establish some level of positive trust (no mistrust) then she would recognize the potential mate who was best for her. And true to form, this did happen over the next year.

As Melissa demonstrated, sometimes the hardest part of truly living is letting go! Sexual relations involve to sets of personalities, therefore two sets of trusting!

CHAPTER SUMMARY -- KEY POINTS

1) The Electra complex was revolutionary in the sense that young females were said to have this unconscious sexual desire for their fathers which eventually turned into learning about the concept of femininity through their mothers and the special relationship with their fathers.

2) Children who are/feel rejected by their mothers are more likely to develop difficulties in creating secure relationships later in life.

3) Gender differences exist in all aspects of society and in most cultures. Right or wrong they are alive and continue to come to a medium ground or get worse in separating genders further.

4) Many people, especially men confuse intimacy with touch feeling. This is where men get led down the garden path to getting things wrong when it comes to intimacy. Intimacy is about feeling and expressing emotion.

5) The expectations of women are the opposite of men, traditionally speaking, as they are taught emotions and intimacy.

CHAPTER FOUR

WHY IT

HAPPENS!

If you want to understand the causes that existed in the past, look at the results as they are manifested in the present. And if you want to understand what results will be manifested in the future, look at the causes that exist in the present.

BUDDHIST QUOTE

When it comes to failing and/or failed relationships, do we really know why anything happens? In all cases the female births the child. This female is the child's mother. Whether a biological mother is in the child's life or some other woman takes the role, there is a woman who is in the child's life. So, the first woman a child grows up with and begins to learn the concept of love and admiration from, is its mother (biological or other). If the boy's mother is not his biological mother the switch has to take place at a very young age, perhaps before age three. It is very important to note that the Madonna complex is not something that develops later in life. It develops quite early in gender identity in children and later in sexual identity in teens. For consideration, the man who loses interest in his wife at fifty, does not have the Madonna complex. He may have relationship issues, hormonal problems, health issues, or other identity/intrapersonal crises going on, however he does not have Madonna complex happening!

With the exception of abusive mothers and mothers where there is an obvious dysfunctional relationship, his mother becomes the worshipped (even in some cases where there is extreme dysfunction the son still holds a bizarre fascination for his mother). After his mother, the woman that the son holds the greatest esteem for should be like his mother. This is also one of the reasons why people always say 'ask a man about his relationship with his mother'. If a woman ever wanted to know how a potential husband will treat her, sign up for a bunch of family functions his family is participating in and watch how he interacts with his mother!

Generally women are categorized by men who possess the Madonna complex in one of two ways:

1) The woman he wants as his girlfriend and potentially his future wife, and;

2) The woman he just wants to have sex with, perhaps the more perverse the better. In this case there is no real intimacy and no real connection. The relationship is built on casual disconnected sex!

In our society boys do not grow up with the conscious notion that they want to have sex with their mother. However, men with this complex do indeed connect the two unconsciously. Their mother is deemed respectable. He or she would never "degrade" herself because she is his mother. He learns to have a great respect for his mother as a woman, primary caregiver and embodiment for what women should be in the real world. Eventually, he seeks attributes his mother has reflected, as being characteristic of women in general, in his future wife.

The psyche of men may become compromised when he starts to perceive women in the world outside of his mother. Perhaps uncertainty starts to surface in his mind in what he should be looking for in a woman versus what he is looking at. What happens when he becomes attracted to the woman who wears the tight dress, high heel shoes and whatever else paraphernalia she is engrossed in, which makes her extremely sexually desirable to him, even though she is all wrong for him? If he wants a serious relationship with someone who is like his mother he cannot allow himself to become enthralled with this type of woman because she is the "whore". She is symbolic of sex rather than a potential mother -- the mother of his kids! Herein the obvious problem starts, especially given the fact that men are highly visual creatures. He wants to have sex with the "whore" but he knows he should marry the "Madonna". In his mind the two cannot co-exist. Men with the Madonna complex are trapped in dichotomous thinking; Women are either purely good, or women are purely evil (raunchy). Worst of all, when men think in such polarized terms, it is because they view life in general through these polarized lenses. The ramifications of this can prove detrimental down the road in his relationships or marriage. Why? Because he believes he needs one woman for each aspect of his personality -- the child bearer and the whore!

Picture if you will a little angel on one shoulder and a little devil on the other. The angel represents rationality while the devil represents temptation. In terms of the Madonna complex, the angel is on alert for wife/maternal quality women while the devil is lusting after naughty women. Since this war goes on within his mind, perhaps for years, even decades, he needs to feed both alter egos (extreme good and extreme bad). How is this accomplished? Easy! He picks the centerpiece/cornerstone woman to be his wife and he selects "fringe" women to be his mistresses or sexual distractions.

It's interesting to examine the domain of battered women syndrome. Often times Peter is asked in lectures and radio/TV shows, "Why do women repeatedly go back to their abusive and/or cheating spouses?" The answer is they possess dual aspects of their relationship personalities: good self and bad self (refer to David Celani's book *Illusion of Love*). The good self is the part that a woman feels makes her worthy and lovable. When her spouse is not beating her or cheating, then she is a "good" wife/woman. On the other hand, when her mate is beating/cheating her, then that must mean she is not a good wife/woman and that must make her bad. In order to survive, facilitate and be an active participant in the cycle of abuse in her marriage/relationship, a woman creates these two selves, good and bad, to explain what is occurring.

Men with Madonna complex also possess these two types of selves. Their selves are created/perpetuated to deal with the inner struggle that goes on inside his own mind. If you will, he possesses a saint versus sinner mentality. The "saint" aspect (good self) is for being a good husband, treating his wife virtuously and being the upstanding father and member of the community he wants people to believe he is. In fact, he really truly wants to be this upstanding person he projects outward. Then comes the dark half -- the sinner! This is the naughty, nasty and perverted side of him he wishes to act out. He was taught or led to believe it is okay to vent and act out these fantasies because there are "dirty" women who fulfill these desires. He engages in perverse acts with them, he keeps his wife virtue intact and preserves the sanctity of his marriage. For him, the good self upholds the virtues of the marriage/wife and the bad self acts outside of the marriage to prevent the "dark side" of him from creeping into his marriage/wife. In some bizarre way, he believes that by cheating he won't pass on this "disease" or filth onto his wife!

A man that does not have the Madonna complex understands that women (and people for that matter) can have a dual nature. For example a woman can possess both sides to her personality. She can be the "good girl" or the Madonna, but she can also be the "bad girl" the whore. And she can balance it very well in not only her world but the man's world as well. In this regard, a man's two selves, "good" and "bad" can co-exist within him with no turmoil and he can be the "good" stand up man in the family/marriage as well as being "bad" in the bedroom with his wife because he knows she understands sex is meant to be fun!

JACK'S MARITAL STORY - A CASE STUDY

Jack is a forty-four year old man who states he married the woman of his dreams. Jack is confused about why he does not want to have sex with his wife. Jack clearly states that he strives for his wife's affection and approval but has no interest in her sexually.

When Jack was questioned about his relationship with his mother, he stated that he always felt (and still does feel) the need for her approval. Jack continues to support his mother, which also causes an issue in his marriage. Jack states he has a sex drive because he fantasizes about having sex with the porn stars that he watches on his computer. Jack masturbates to the women in the porn and states that his arousal is intense. Jack states he feels close to having an affair on his wife because he needs to have sex. Jack states his wife wants to have sex but he just doesn't have an interest. Jack also states that his wife is very aggressive in the "bedroom".

When Jack was asked about the types of porn movies he watches and the types of women in them he claimed to prefer passive female stars. When asked about the woman's passivity, he claimed to prefer women who were submissive to the whims of the male stars in the films.
Jack was also asked if this is how he would prefer his wife to be in the bedroom as he quickly answered "yes"! The idea of a woman being more powerful than him really bothered him. In terms of a woman's sexuality, he believed he should be the more dominant one. He should be the initiator, aggressor and finisher.

Growing up he watched how his mother ruled the house. His father was away on business quite a bit so his mother for all intents and purposes played both roles -- mother and father. Eventually his parents split as his father couldn't stand the perfectionist expectations placed on him by his mother. When his father left for good, Jack was 12 and at that point, being an only child he found he became the target of his mother's domination. Furthermore, his mother never dated and began all men as wimps and losers. Jack vowed to never get married, or ever date a woman like his mother. As an adult before he had a chance to blink and clear his throat he realized he had not only dated a woman like his mother, but was also married to one and had a daughter!

When asked, "Does your wife scare or intimidate you?" Jack responds, "As stupid a question that is, I think she does!" Jack felt like he was married to his mother and this drove him crazy! Not having sex was enough to drive him insane, but realizing he married in essence a younger version of his mother made him feel like he was going over the edge! What in the world was he thinking when he chose to date and eventually marry her?

The above case of Jack is interesting because it shows something very clearly with regard to the development of the Madonna complex. Jack's mother is someone whom Jack has always sought approval from which is also transferred to his wife. In addition, Jack's wife is very aggressive in sex, when Jack does not see his mother that way. Therefore, two women who Jack desperately seeks approval from, are not seen in the same way. One is the Madonna (his mother) and the other is both (the Madonna and the whore). For Jack this does not translate well. The result is a disinterest in sexual desire for his wife. Furthermore, it equates with intimidation for Jack. The idea of his wife, who is so much like his mother being the aggressor in the bedroom just feels so wrong to him!

It is also important to mention that a man who has the Madonna complex wants his wife or girlfriend to be a lady in front of his family and friends, as well as lady woman in the bedroom. A man with this complex has a deep rooted thinking disorder where he desires a "lady" all the way around! The whore on the other hand is reserved for his dark side -- the "other woman", to appease his perverse, sexual hunger. Love and sex do not match up for a man seeing the world through the lenses of the Madonna complex. Most often sex is a dirty act because he does not view his mother as having a sexual nature. For all intents and purposes she is "just" a mom -- asexual! Growing up she took care of his needs and his needs were not sexual at that point. Here's something to think about... Try to picture in your mind your parents having sex. Nasty, scary, horrific image, right? No one wants to picture that, well at least unless you are into the whole Oedipus complex delusional way of thinking. With that said, boys later becoming young men don't want to picture their mothers in that vein!

The way a man with the Madonna complex has been reared has socialized him into compartmentalizing women. He believes that there is no one as sacred as his mother. He believes women are either righteous creatures or whores. Furthermore, there is a great distrust of women with men who have this complex. Often times they put the woman they are with, to a test to see who they are getting. (Keep in mind that this complex can be seen as early as puberty). The test can be seen as a way to see if the female fits within one of two categories, sexual play thing, or wife material. If she proves to be "too easy", then that places her in the former category of play toy. Conversely, if he has to work hard to get her affections, or she won't put out unless there is a commitment, then she is definitely girlfriend and/or marriage material.

In the beginning, he may be very sexually active and seek out the "bad girl". He will play with her for a time but eventually he realizes he will have to stop it because she is not good for him. Instead the light goes on in his head and he will turn his attention to finding his Madonna. The Madonna will replace his physical intimacy needs with more noble emotional needs that resemble those needs he had met as an infant, child, teen and perhaps young adult by his mother. Basically, he needs a younger version of his mother to mother his children as well as himself!

When the boundaries become enmeshed for a man who views his wife and mother in the same light, it spells disaster. In fact, when you ask a married woman whose husband is more loyal to his mother than her, she often times feels like "the other woman"... The mistress! Conversely, she might view his mother as the mistress, the woman he is cheating with, emotionally.

Then there is the platonic relationship a man has with his mother that raises his wife's dander! Of course all men who have mothers have "platonic" relationships with their mothers, but there are those who have platonic relationships with their mothers which compete and infringe upon their relationships with their wives.

Some women report that even though they are married, they rarely see their husbands because he is always at his mother's house or has to take her out all of the time. Furthermore, some report that since marrying their husband, he still needs to go to his mother's house for lunch or dinner one or more times a week. What perturbs his wife even more is that she is not even invited!

What happens in a more "tamed" version of the Madonna complex is some men develop a serious relationship with their mothers based on obligation, habit and/or intense fascination. Even when they leave their mothers to go to their girlfriends or wives, their mothers are always a part of the picture, a big picture!

The attributes of this man's mother usually fit the following criteria which she directly instigates or vicariously achieves through his thought process (the psychological parent - representation of her he carries with him in his mind):

1) Overbearing - Whatever she says, goes.

2) Managing - She continues to manage her son's life even though he is an

adult.

3) Goodness of fit - No woman will ever be good enough for her son.

4) Competition - Even when he does date or marry, his mother creates competition with his mate for his affection.

5) Transference - He looks for his wife to be as good as his mother and

demands that she provide for him like his mother.

6) Psychological parent guilt/shame - When he is away from his mother for   prolonged   periods,   he feels guilty and needs to "check" in with her.

We interviewed women who identified this type of man (Madonna complex). They helped us create the former attributes which we just listed. We found women who reported to us, along with some men, that this was more apparent in certain European and Asian cultures.

In his books *Penis Envy* and *Fast Food Dating Your 2 Cents*, Peter interviewed over a thousand women and found nearly the exact same correlations we found for this book. The women interviewed made two strong analogies which would have made Sigmund Freud proud. First, some claimed their men, or the men they had dated in the past, seemed literally connected to their mothers as if the umbilical cord had never been severed. Second, the feeding component and running back to their mothers was almost like something taken right out of Freud's first two Psychosexual stages; ORAL and ANAL. According to Freud, the Oral stage obviously focussed on the breast (breast feeding) and teething. In this case, the men exchanged the breast (so we would hope) for mom's home cooked meals. The breast/teething is a babies way to bond and form its first security to its mother. Obviously this first security/bonding still exists in some men where they feel the need or obligation to be fed by their mothers only (home cooked meals).

Similarly, Freud's second stage Anal, focuses on the ability of the infant to control their world by going potty. They can keep it in or excrete it and either way they get their mother's attention. Sometimes she needs to change them because he did something "bad" in his pants. As a grown man, whenever he does something wrong, he runs to his mother to fix things... Change him. This couldn't be more indicative in his marriage whenever he gets into a fight with his wife. Where does he go? He runs to mother!

Several women reported that whenever their husbands had fights/disagreements with them, especially over their children, his mother was the first person he ran to. We had some women assert that a man is "always married to his mother for better or for worse!". His mother has set the bar at how a woman in his life should be, act and treat him. If and when the two do not match up, it has the potential to lead to inner conflict for which he may seek escape -- to his mother, another woman, work addiction, sports addictions, pornography, alcohol, drugs, gambling, etc.

We will close out this chapter with an interesting case study demonstrating how a man with the Madonna complex is not capable of serving two women -- wife and mother equally.

SUSAN AND THOMAS -- THE MADONNA/WHORE MARRIAGE: A CASE STUDY

Susan and Thomas married at age nineteen. Susan had been with a few other males but those relationships did not get consummated. When Susan met Thomas the two hit it off. They enjoyed the same things; they laughed a lot and they appeared to have the same goals!

Susan reported thinking Thomas's mother was both cold and over protective when she met her a few times. She also remembers Thomas trying to please his mother on countless occasions. Thomas would suffer when he felt as though his mother was not pleased.

Susan even thought it was pathetic to see a "man" in a large physical body grovelling and begging his mother like a little child!

Susan stated that Thomas wanted to have sex and was quite pushy in the beginning but they waited about eight months before they had intercourse. After the first year Thomas proposed marriage to Susan. Everything started out pretty good in the beginning. Thomas has always been into smoking weed and trying other drugs but nothing too intense. Over the next couple of years his drug use got worse. Susan worried about whether or not their marriage would last! She took the pill and continued to stay on it because she did not want to get pregnant. She realized Thomas was not responsible enough to be a father.

Now both age twenty-eight, Susan and Thomas have not had sex for three years. Before that, Susan reports Thomas losing all interest in sex! She wondered if the abuse of drugs had caused Thomas to become impotent and reduce his testosterone levels. She forced him to see his doctor. Thomas's testosterone levels were normal and there was no diagnosis of disease!

The sexless marriage only got worse. The couple fought more and Thomas got into more hardcore drugs. At this time his relationship with his mother also bottomed out. For the last five years they had been speaking very little. She had rejected him first for his choice of marrying Susan and now for his drug use/abuse. When his drugging got worse, Thomas' mother cut him off all together! This totally drove him over the edge and was now a full-blown addict!

Susan fought with him to get help for his addiction. He rejected her. She felt helpless and rejected. She felt like she didn't matter! Because of the lack of sex in the marriage Susan decided to have an affair to satisfy her needs of being wanted by a man. The guilt of the affair consumed Susan with hatred for both Thomas and herself. She made one last ditch effort to help Thomas and save their marriage.

She organized an intervention, gathering mutual friends and family members. Thomas' mother would not participate. When Thomas was confronted by members at the intervention it enraged him. Not seeing his mother there really hurt as well. She didn't care! Even though the intervention was not a success, Thomas did get into a detox/treatment program but that only lasted for a week before he started using again.

Susan couldn't stand anymore rejection and guilt. Eventually she filed for divorce and moved out of the area. She went back to school and started a new life. Thomas eventually went into a 30 day residential program and got the help he needed. There he learned about the acceptance/rejection issues surrounding him. He learned about the components which comprise the Madonna complex. He is still living one day at a time and learning to find his place in the world, independent of his mother!

CHAPTER SUMMARY -- KEY POINTS

1) A man that does not have the Madonna complex understands that women can have a dual nature. The same woman can be both; nice in the real world and naughty in the bedroom.

2) The way a man with the Madonna complex has been reared has socialized him into compartmentalizing women. He believes his mother is the standard of excellence or shame for what a woman is.

3) Eventually any man possessing the Madonna complex needs a younger version of his mother (his wife or girlfriend) to mother his children as well as himself. His mate is measured against and compared to his mother.

4) Some men develop a serious relationship with their mothers based on obligation, habit and/or intense fascination. They have a hard time letting go even when they are married.

5) The Madonna complex has the potential to lead to inner conflict for which a man may seek escape through substance use/abuse.

CHAPTER FIVE

SOCIETAL

INFLUENCES

A man's faults all conform to his type of mind. Observe his faults and you may know his virtues.

CHINESE PROVERB

Society always has and always will influence it's people. Societal influences run very deep in most cultures and have the propensity, whether right or wrong, to influence how people think. Thousands of years of thinking a certain way does not change overnight. In fact, it is more likely to evolve or flourish in different ways.

In Western society as well as many others, sex is visually and emotionally free with few exceptions. We are inundated by a plethora of "sex". Whenever anyone wants it, they are most likely to find it in one form or another. Sex is everywhere from billboards to magazine ads, to television and movies, to music... It's virtually everywhere! With virtual technology continuing to grow leaps and bounds yearly, it literally is everywhere. As humans, we are influenced heavily through the society in the realms of religion, tradition, and customs.

From a theoretical perspective Albert Bandura's Social Learning Theory postulates that we learn through observation of others, i.e. observational learning. The idea is if people observe positive outcomes or rewards (behaviour) they may be more likely to behave in that way, essentially model the behaviour. It is a monkey-see/monkey-do mentality!

The origins of social learning theory posits that we learn on the presumption of four different aspects of imitation/modeling:

1. Being in close contact with other people or a person who captures our attention.

2. Modeling someone we perceive as superior to us or modeling someone who is demonstrating a superior behaviour.

3. The necessity to understand the concepts that we are imitating or modeling so that we at least have some semblance in our own minds why we are doing something, even if it only makes minimal sense to us.

4. Choosing someone we perceive as a good role model who demonstrates a behaviour/idealism which we would like to recapitulate, whether it is right or wrong.

When you put all four aspects intact, an individual starts to become untrue to their identity. If we are mere models of other human beings can true individuality actually exist?

How does this play into the Madonna complex? When we look at famous people in the media -- people who we admire, people who we would like to be more like, people whom life seems superb while ours is just a mere existence, then we begin to show signs of this imitation behaviour. We become carbon copies for how we see others behaving. Early in our lives, we do not have the critical sensors built into our minds to discern abstract thoughts. We rely solely on the decisions, actions and personalities of those we perceive as prime role models.

It is fascinating how many kids and youth growing up emulate celebrities and sports icons. Since the majority of marriages today result in divorce and the average time parents spend effectively communicating with their children daily is 2 1/2 to 4 1/2 minutes, is it any wonder why kids look outside their homes, or the T.V., big screen and Internet, for role models? Interestingly, before technology came along there was really only radio, books and records with limited television and movies. We have come a long way technologically, but not a long way in terms of modeling.

In our society people play roles. Furthermore the people playing these roles come from different personalities -- no two individual personalities are the same. The experiences leading to our thought processes, which eventually trigger our feeling states, come about from different socialization processes. Moreover, even though two people can be brought up in the exact same environments, at the exact same time and be identical twins, their personalities still differ. How is that possible? Simply their perceptions of the experiences which occurred at the same time for both of them differ. This is what makes individuals unique.

The best way to demonstrate how socialization affects everyone is to realize there is a beginning and an end to the process. Every socialization process always starts out with an event, whether consciously or unconsciously perceived, and a mindset created around those perceptions which in turn lead to a way of becoming.

Here is a diagram which best describe the series of events as they flow from beginning to end:

EVENT OCCURS -->PERCEPTION OF EVENT-->I THINK-->I FEEL-->I ACT--> I BECOME

First the *event occurs*. It might have been intentional or by chance. At this point an event is nothing outside of itself if no one is there to perceive it. It's like the analogy of a "tree falling in the forest", in that if no one is there to witness and hear it happening, does it actually make a sound? The same is true for events as a whole. You need to see it, hear about it or experience it in some form to give it meaning.

Once the event has occurred, you need to interpret it based on a collection of perceptions and memories from previous experiences that were nearly identical, similar as well as contrast them to different situations. The mind is an amazing central processing unit that it does this entire process in microseconds. Once it compares and contrasts all memories/experiences from the past, it makes a final judgement on this immediate experience and that becomes the *perception of the event*.

When we start to impress former perceptions, memories and experiences into our minds (conscious and unconscious) we have a file to tap into in terms of how we should *think* about those events. In order to truly experience anything in life, we have to think about it. Many of us use stereotypes which are shortcuts to perceptions to think about things. Unfortunately, stereotypes are often times negative and a lazy way of thinking. Instead of experiencing the event completely and letting it engulf our perceptions, we sometimes experience just a little and then form an opinion based on previous experiences and thought processes. Our thought processing becomes placed on autopilot and we respond like conditioned rats in a maze. It's imperative to experience as much or all of the event as possible and form a new opinion based on our crystallized memory perceptions!

Then comes the feeling part. Most people believe they "just feel", or they feel before they think. That is impossible! You can't feel something unless you think that feeling into being. You can't feel by proxy. If you are angry, you are angry because you thought about something that made you angry. Furthermore, just the fact that a terrible event happened can't make you angry unless you attach an "angry" label to that event through thinking, which derive their possibilities from the memories of former, similar events. You feel the way you do because you think the way that you do!

After you start feeling a certain way, you are most likely to *act* accordingly. When was the last time you saw an extremely joyful person acting out their joy by doing angry things? If they were, then no doubt they were probably certifiably loony tunes!

It's interesting that how we feel can sometimes become habitual. The reason it becomes habitual is because of the mind -- it operates on cruise control and gets stuck in chains of patterned thinking. Unfortunately, most people spend most of their thought stores focussing on negative things which leads them to feeling down, depressed or anxious.

Once you continually think, feel and act a certain way, you are then set up to *become* the sum of those by-products. If you are always angry then you are most likely to appear like an angry person because you have become an angry person!

In law there is an interesting saying that possession is 9/10ths of the law. In the world of thinking, feeling, acting and becoming, you might say that perception is 9/10ths of the experience. If this is the case, then society is roughly 1/10th or just responsible for 10% of who and what we are! Yes, society can influence people, but at the end of the day it is what they are allowing in and how they go about censoring or not censoring things, that determine what will become of them.

TONY'S PUSHING-PULLING TENDANCIES - A CASE STUDY

Tony has what is called Independent Personality Disorder. It is more common in males. Tony is an individual who always exaggerates his sense of sureness and personal power. Whenever he is in a relationship, he emphasizes his lack of need for others. He constantly tells his girlfriends he is able to live without others forever. Well, this happens while his mate is still in his life.

Tony learned from his father early on that no man should ever become dependent or rely on a woman. he witnessed this growing up as he watched his parents. His mother often demonstrated in her behaviour that she was less than equal to his father and that her job in the marriage was just that... A job -- cook, clean, make babies and then raise those babies. Tony's father led Tony to believe that if he got too close to women they would use and abuse him. They would use him for his money and then leave him. Some would try to trap him by getting pregnant and then he would be stuck with them. At an early age Tony made a vow never to marry or really fall in love with a woman. Tony didn't realize that falling in love is often times not a choice but loving someone and staying with them, is!

Tony best characterized his behaviour in his relationships as desperate. Whenever Tony felt his relationship slipping away, he would become obsessed with the need to control the object of his jealousy, his mate. He was constantly driven by his anger which was caused by an irrational fear of being abandoned. You see, by the time Tony was ten, his mother packed up and left not only their home and marriage, but also the country and went back to the Middle East. This made his father more irate than sad. This confused Tony and his younger brother somewhat!

As Tony became as adolescent, he developed very distorted thoughts about what love is. From the time he started dating he had always been a "pusher-puller" in all his relationships. The closer someone got to Tony, the more he would withdraw and push them away. When they finally started to take his cue and decided to leave him, he would beg them to come back and give him another chance. This method of operating in his relationships has plagued Tony for nearly 20 years now. At 36 years of age, he is finally seeking professional counselling to try and change his approach to relationships.

In this situation involving Tony, you can see how his perceptions based on how his father treated his mother led him to treat the women in his own life. His method of operation was to constantly self-destruct in the relationships he was in, and then try to repair them. Ironically, his mother never returned to the marriage or family but he remembers how much his father pleaded over the phone, in letters, flying to the Middle East as he tried to "fix things".

Where does society come into play, if it does at all? Since women are traditionally viewed as the weaker of the two sexes, and the "used", what is the norm for societies outlook on this?

When examining the Madonna complex we have to take a close look at the role of the "virtuous wife" and the role of the "whore." Traditionally, in most cultures, religion sets the standards for how a wife is to behave in a marriage. Basically if she could practice two important domestic requirements, she would succeed at being a wife. First, it's her role of staying faithful/monogamous to her husband (even if she's in a polygamous marriage) and providing him with children. Second, she's the manager of the house -- cooking, cleaning and making sure everyone is taken care of.

Why the heck would any woman want to sign up for this? In the old days, it was very important for women to marry because of their economic status. Women without husbands were usually poor and undesirable. The marriage gave them status in relation to their husbands. Why do you think wives traditionally took on their husband's surname and dropped their own?

Regarding sex, the wife was to engage in sexual relations with her husband for the purpose of procreation. She was not to enjoy sex but rather enjoy making her husband happy and relaxed. Guess who got to enjoy the foreplay? Is it any wonder today women often times complain most men don't want to have foreplay, or it's all "wham, bam and thank you ma'am!". When you think about it, traditionally women have been the pleasers, appeasers and servers. Just as they are better at communicating their emotions, they are also more in touch with the sexuality of their bodies. This is something society taught early on and still continues today, even though today's woman is becoming more dominant sexually and saying, "Give me my foreplay first bud or you ain't getting any!"

Even though traditional thinking has been amended to involve today's wives as equals in marriages in most societies, old habits still die hard! In many cultures today, women still marry for companionship and love. It is still expected for women to marry or they are viewed as greater failures than men. In fact, women who don't marry are often referred to as "spinsters" and "wallflowers"! Can you find any good connotations associated with those descriptors?

Conversely, men who don't marry are considered "eligible bachelors", "still playing the field", "not ready to settle down", etc. You get the point! Single men can play the field till the cows come home and never be put out to pasture!

The opposite also exists as well. Women who do marry and get divorced one or more times get the negative connotation of being "used goods" or "all used up" especially if she has had children. Divorced men on the other hand who have fathered children are "sewing their seeds". Therefore, at the end of the day, it's better for a woman to get married and stay married no matter how miserable she is. On the other hand, men can be happy if they are single, if they are married or if they get a divorce. At least that is the stigma society has placed on it. Remember that perceptions are 90% of the experience, and from societal perspective this means status... Image is everything!

Currently in North America and in some countries in Europe, divorce rates are anywhere from 40-50%. That means that one in two marriages fail! Some scholars point out that such high rates in divorce exist because of the aforementioned reasons... People, particularly women, getting married for all the wrong reasons. Many still believe it is the right thing to do to gain their status in adulthood. Today, people can get divorced for incompatibility and/or irreconcilable differences. The rule that once were the cornerstones for divorce, cruelty and infidelity, have become more trite.

Recently in Canada, it was reported that for the first time since anyone could remember, there were more single adults than married adults. Today there is a huge spike in single parent (usually the mother) families. Furthermore, more women are getting married and not having children. Even though married, they have opted for new careers in the real world which don't involve raising kids and managing a house. They are equal to men in the work world on many parts of the globe and men have been forced to re-examine their career statuses and once held powers. Wives also can and do enjoy sex and can be the sexual aggressors. While it is true that many men enjoy this sexual aggression/initiative on their wives' part, there are still many who do not, particularly who are "old school" or who are plagued by the Madonna complex.

The concept of "whore" refers to sexual promiscuity. When you trace the word back in history, it is often associated with "prostitute". You can trace this all the way back to biblical times. Throughout history and different cultures, the position of being a prostitute was accepted. As Christianity grew throughout the world over the centuries, the church defined all sexual promiscuity as wrong and evil. Sex was for the purpose of procreation within the marriage and sexual promiscuity inside the marriage (between husband and wife) in some stern religions was also forbidden. Interestingly, when you look back at the history of prostitution, often times wives and prostitutes (a.k.a. concubines) lived in the same house together with the wife's husband. All of these women had legal rights and equal status.

Interestingly the historical significance of having both the wife and concubine (sex slave/whore) in the same house somewhat set the polarity for Marianismo and Misogyny. Obviously the wife held the good, clean whole virtues of the Marianismo. She was expected to create offspring that would keep her husband's gene pool/family name alive and going forward. On the other hand, concubines/whores played the misogyny roles. They were the dirty women who were the receptors for a husband's animalistic, sexual tensions which had nothing to do with love. Any sex he had therefore was basically viewed as a cleansing or a release. Interestingly today, there are establishments operated by women called "rub and tugs" which provide release! Men pay money to attend these places in order to release tensions perhaps caused by his married life, fatherhood or work. Then again, it just might be his strong animalistic drive that perpetuates these places to exist!

What is extremely fascinating is at one point in time both wives and whores lived together and had the same legalities. In essence, the wife served her role and the whore(s) served her role within the same house. Today, if a husband is caught cheating, legalities do come into play and these are not the same legalities both the wife and mistress share. The wife usually takes it all!

FRANK'S FASCINTATION WITH LARGE BREASTS - A CASE STUDY

Frank and Martha have been married for 5 years. Both of them felt it was late in their life to get married. Frank was 41 years old and Martha was 38 years of age. Frank and Martha had what was described by both as an average sex life before Martha got pregnant with their now three year old child. They reported having sex about once a week prior to the birth of their son. Martha wanted to have sex more than Frank and the couple reported arguing often over the notion that there was not enough sex in their marriage.

For the last three years, since the birth of their son they engage in sex on average only twice a year.

Martha states that she has done everything such as buying sexy lingerie, talking dirty to Frank, and even took classes in belly dancing and the art of strip tease. This made no difference at all! In fact, Martha states that Frank calls her stupid and accuses her of looking and acting like a whore.

Martha feels extremely rejected and has not tried to entice her husband into sexual relations anymore because of the rejection and the blow she has taken to her self esteem. Frank states he has an interest in sex but just can't seem to desire his Martha the way he engages fantasies toward other women.

Frank was asked what type of woman he desired. What he desired was a very large-breasted blonde woman. Ironically, Martha is not far from the picture that Frank painted, yet he did not want to have sex with her!

Martha recalls one time in an argument that Frank yelled "start acting like a respectable wife!" What Frank really meant was for her to be non-sexual and if and when he wanted sex with her, then he would notify her.

Frank wanted a woman who looked like his wife to have sex with! He was already married to the woman he fantasized about in the looks department. The problem was that Martha was the mother of their child and she spoke and acted according to her own mind. The woman in Frank's fantasy had no voice of her own, only what Frank gave her.

What Frank didn't realize is that often times fantasies are just that... Fantasies! In the real world they often times do not measure up to the extremely high expectations people have. What if Frank cheated on Martha with the buxom blonde he fantasized about, only to learn afterwards that it wasn't worth the cost of his marriage?

Frank did go to a massage parlour (rub and tug) and had a young blonde perform masturbation on him. He didn't enjoy the experience as he hoped or thought he would. In fact, he couldn't wait for it to end. He never did tell his wife about it after it happened, but he did decide to try engaging Martha in sex more often.

In the beginning Martha thought something was "up", and that Frank acted out of guilt. As to what he was guilty about, she chose not to care as long as it seemed sex was back in their marriage.

Their marriage did not become great, but it became better than it had been in years.

The most inexperienced women (and most men) consider sex and love to go hand and hand. The traditional message that good girls don't have sex until they marry, while bad girls do. Marriage is for good girls who do the right things with their sexuality!

With the Madonna complex, sex after marriage defiles the expectations of what a wife is suppose to be and often times the relationship develops major functional issues. Infidelity often occurs because of sex and intimacy issues within the marriage. A husband seeks sex with a "whore", while a wife seeks sex with someone who is going to meet her needs emotionally -- Intimacy!

In nearly every society past and present, the "mother" is usually not viewed as "sexy" or sexual by nature. Certainly she had to engage in sex to get pregnant, that is unless she was Madonna herself! Moreover, once the mother has done her job and made babies, societal influence can kick in and this is when a sexless marriage begins. These influences become indicative of the Madonna complex. One example is that when children are born the mother needs to be nurturing and take on all the responsibility to raise healthy stable kids -- she has no time to be sexual. Interestingly, it was only recently that terms like cougar (older women/moms) and MILF (Moms I'd Like to bleep -- four letter super adjective starting with "F" and ending in "K") that have painted mothers as being sexy and sexual beings. There are now handfuls of websites on-line (mostly) porn depicting these types of women for men to get their jolly's off on -- someone's mother or someone else's wife! Why can't every married man just enjoy his own wife for crying out loud?

We interviewed a gentleman named Geoff about the topic of the Madonna Complex: and this was what he had to say:

"I don't have the Madonna complex (at least not that I know of) but I can see how it is possible. I'm not married but I expect my girlfriend to act like a "good girl (if that's what you want to call it)" in public and around my friends. I want her to be a freak in the bedroom though. I can see how a guy wouldn't want to have sex with his child's mother. She is just different as a mother I suppose for some! I don't think I'll be like that but I can definitely see how it's possible."

Another Male named Mike said this:

"Women can be both. That is a beautiful thing. They can be the nice girl but they can also be the bad girl. I want a girl that has both these qualities. I don't know what guy wouldn't. Who doesn't want to have

great sex with the person that they marry? You may be spending the rest of your life with that person so it better be good or at least be workable to make it better!"

James stated:

" I don't really know how I feel about sexual women. Where did they learn the behaviour from? Maybe I want someone to marry that doesn't have a lot of experience. I don't want to think of her having sex with other dudes. Shouldn't women be more pure -- your potential wife I mean?"

From these three interviews who do you think exemplifies attributes of the Madonna complex. We'll give you a hint... It's not the first two!

JANE IS JUST FED UP! - A CASE STUDY

Jane is so tired and fed up with being misunderstood by men. The last three relationships she had, started out really well and it seemed to her and each of her mates that they had so much to talk about every time. As the relationships progressed, it seemed to her the men she chose became less tolerant of her requests to communicate at deeper intimate levels. In fact, the more she tried to get them to open up, it seemed the more they tended to raise their voices and almost yell at her. She wasn't deaf! Also, she was not implying they were hard of hearing. It seemed they just weren't listening to what she was saying. When she asked them about their "future" together, they would respond about "living one day at a time" and "no rush to jump into anything too serious". This confused her greatly because in the beginning, it was they who had pursued her and literally begged her to marry them. Now, that they knew they had her affection, the tables had changed. Was Jane really expecting too much from her mates? Had her mates deceived her into making her believe they were something they really weren't? Are they able and willing to understand her point of view and where she is coming from? How can they start out being so emotionally hot, only to have their communicative emotions dwindle to a flicker? Finally, what also caught Jane's attention was the fact that when she had enough and was ready to bail from the relationship, her mates would come on emotionally strong and "promise" to love her more and of course "change". They would be the type of communicator Jane wanted them to be! Well, do you think this change is possible after the many years of who and what they are? Should Jane wait or hope for them to change into what she wants them to be? If they

change for Jane, is it because they really love her, or is it more out of fear of losing what they want?

Traditionally men were encouraged to be the superior gender in relationships. If you will, they held "upman-ship", "hand" or power in the relationship. Often times when a man feels his relationship is slipping away, or that his mate is on the verge of leaving the relationship, he is willing to swallow his pride, grovel for mercy and relinquish his power in relationship -- at least until he "wins" her back/over and can regain control. The case study involving Jane demonstrates this. Perhaps this is the only time a man's perception of the dichotomy of "virtuous" versus "whore" gets diverted in the Madonna complex. The only thing he focuses on is not getting rejected and losing his mate.

CHAPTER SUMMARY - KEY POINTS

1) Societal influences run very deep in most cultures and influence how people think. Thousands of years of thinking a certain way does not change overnight.

2) Albert Bandura's *Social Learning Theory* postulates that we learn through observation of others. It is a monkey-see/monkey-do mentality!

3) Once you continually think, feel and act a certain way, you are then set up to become the sum of those by-products.

4) In many cultures today, women still marry for companionship and love. It is still expected for women to marry or they are viewed as greater failures than men.

5) With the Madonna complex, sex after marriage defiles the expectations of what a wife is suppose to be, leading to major functional issues. Infidelity often occurs because of sex and intimacy issues within the marriage.

CHAPTER SIX

MEDIA
INFLUENCES
ON PORN ADDICTIONS

A widespread taste for pornography means that nature is alerting us to some threat of extinction.

J.G. Ballard

If someone came up to you and asked you if you knew where to find some form of pornography as soon as possible, how hard would it be for you to satisfy their desire? Would you know where to look immediately? If you had your Blackberry or I-phone with you, would you have to look any further than that? Simply put, porn or some form of it, is literally everywhere now, even on our own possession with only a few presses of a tiny keyboard!

Earlier in this book we mentioned that there are over 100 million pages on the Internet devoted to porn. We're guessing since we printed those words, the number of pages has further increased!

For those of you old enough, do you remember the time when porn could only be found in adult only stores or magazine/cigarette stores? Funny, but that wasn't all too long ago. In fact, even before those times, if you wanted to view porn you had to pay to go to an "adult" theatre which featured pornography. Back in the day, porn viewing and enjoyment was pretty much done as discreetly and inconspicuously as possible. Today, there is really nothing too discreet about pornography. With heightened technological and media advancements, pornography is everywhere for viewers who choose to indulge in.

When the Internet came along, it was at that time that ideas for creating and promoting pornography expanded. Furthermore, corporations, small business and individuals jockeyed for opportunities and positions for creating porn on the Internet. Their goal was to reach as great a number of people as possible. Getting their "product/service" to viewers was the hardest part. Getting viewers hooked was like picking off fish in a barrel!

First off, sex sells today as it always has! If you go back to Freud's Life and Death Instinct theories back in the 1800's you will see he was definitely on the money. Freud's Life Instinct was basically about procreation -- sex! One engaged in sex with as many different partners to sow their seeds. Animalistic speaking, it was to keep the species alive and evolving. The Death Instinct was primarily about survival. An organism did whatever it could to stay alive -- Survival of the fittest/strongest!

Think about it for a moment. Freud postulated his theories well before television was a fantasy and radio was just on the cusp of being. The main forms of "media" of the day were art/paintings and of course books. Interestingly, there were many detractors who thought Freud was insane for believing what he was theorizing. They thought he was mad! How dare a psychiatrist assert that humans were nothing more than barbarians in the 1800's, mostly driven by sex and violence? Fast forward to the 21st Century. If you look at Hollywood movies and television, and even books, which ones are the most popular and successful? Those would be the ones containing sex and violence. Sex still sells today, perhaps more than it ever has, because with Wi-Fi technology, it can literally reach the entire masses of the world -- all corners!

Just how can something created for entertainment purposes and in some circumstances for the purpose of "art", be so harmful and addictive? Is it really harmful and can pornography be addictive, or is it just an excuse? Before we answer these questions, the following case study will perhaps shed some degree of light on pornography as addictive.

SEAN'S NAKED TRUTH ABOUT PORN -- A CASE STUDY

I never thought in my wildest imagination that I could or ever would get addicted to porn. Before I knew what hit me, namely my wife threatening to divorce me unless I got help, I was in over my head, constantly spending the better part of my days watching people having sex!

I would say the potential for habit was there all the way back to when I was a teenager. Back in the day I was into nudie magazines just like the next guy. When I started to first get the books either from friends as hand-me-downs, or discreetly buying them in convenience stores, they were more for thrills and arousal. I liked girls very much back then and dated much so I never really got hooked on porn magazines. A buddy of mine and I would also go to the porn theatre sometimes, but it wasn't really for arousal, rather to make fun of the guys in the theatre as well as the stupid movies.

It was in my 20's that I first started to really expose myself to the sex trade. I started frequenting strip clubs more readily. I would go, get aroused and then come home and take care of myself. I was always too shy and afraid to approach a dancer for a sexual favor so I was not really into lap dances. It wasn't long after that I met someone, fell in love with her, dated for a few years before finally marrying her.

Throughout our dating, I watched porn occasionally whenever I was alone. It was enough to get me off, and that was the extent of it. I had a pretty decent sex life with my mate which didn't seem as satisfying the longer we were together. There was no doubt in my mind that I loved her to death and knew she was the only woman I wanted to spend the rest of my life with. If I had to choose between her and having "okay" sex or being single and sleeping around and having great sex, there was no second thoughts... I loved her and wanted her forever!

After we got married, our careers got very hectic and many nights throughout the week we were apart. I worked straight days and my wife worked late evenings. This left me with a lot of time on my hands. And idle hands definitely became evil hands in my world!

I started watching television on channels like Showcase and Bravo as well as some other ethnic networks. The women on the shows that I watched drove me sexually crazy. The nearly-naked or totally naked women on these shows drove me over the edge. It got to the point where I started watching certain shows as masturbation material for myself. After a few months I started to get less aroused by what I was watching and began craving something "stronger". Through dumb-luck I stumbled onto an adult channel that was free! They showed most anything and everything. Before I knew it, I was watching porn every night that my wife worked. When she was home with me, I still craved it. Even when we have sexual relations, I was craving porn and the women I saw in the videos.

It wasn't long after that my wife took steady day hours with her company that we had our evenings together. At first I welcomed the opportunity to have my wife with me. I wanted so bad to stop watching porn. I thought that having her around at night would save me from myself!

Our sex life improved somewhat but not to the standard I had set for myself in my mind. Unless it was a porn star at this point, I don't think any woman would satiate me. My wife became curious at first and then concerned after I suggested experimenting sexually. She wondered "why" I was suggesting such bizarre and perverse sexual acts. Where had I learned them from? She then wondered if I was bored with her and our marriage. This unlocked a bunch of issues and I thought it was best to keep my mouth shut and have vanilla sex with her. It was later that I realized that sex was sex (an act) and that what I called vanilla was only my perception because I had become hooked on all the window-dressing of pornography -- illusion and lies.

It was then that my porn addiction found a new venue... The Internet. It was insane at how much was on there. It was a buffet! I knew it was there, and I had been tempted to play on it. I knew the havoc it could create in my life. Eventually curiosity brought me to the place I most tried to avoid. Before I knew it, I was way in over my head.

I was "using" porn on our desktop computer discreetly. I was using it on my laptop at work. I also figured out how to use it on my Blackberry. I used it whenever I was alone. I would get a cup of coffee and sit in a vacant parking lot and watch porn when my wife was at home. I would leave to go get groceries or pick something up and wind up in the mall parking lot. I would tell myself I would just watch for a few minutes. Those minutes would eventually become a half hour or an hour. My wife would wonder what had taken so long!

Our sex life was next to non-existent. She wanted to, but I didn't anymore. I didn't need her for that. I believed I had something better and more fulfilling. As long as I had a "wife" and I had my porn, everything was complete.

It was one night when I came home from work that my wife appeared very upset. I thought something bad had happened. She looked very distant and dejected. I asked her what was wrong. I will never forget how she got up from her chair looked at me and asked me to follow her in a whisper. She led me to the computer room and sat at the computer. There she started flipping through all the porn sites I was visiting. I was shocked to see them. I didn't know how to clear my browsing history. She had found them. She confronted me.

I remember how I wanted to deny visiting them so badly. I couldn't! A part of me was relieved that I had been caught. Another part worried that she would leave me. And she did threaten to leave me and seek a divorce unless I got help.

At first I denied I had a problem. Even though I knew I had a problem, I told her I could fix it and get it under control on my own. She doubted me.

Again, it was one night after work when I came home to a house full of people -- mostly family members and friends. She had told them what was happening and how I was addicted to porn. I was so embarrassed and angry with her and everyone there. They were there to help me. Before I knew it, they were holding an intervention for me! A friend of a friend was a counsellor and she was there to help out.

In that moment in time I learned how much hurt and harm I had caused to my wife. She was ready to leave me unless I got professional help. I talked with everyone in the house as they expressed their concerns and love for me. Before the night was up, I had agreed to seek counselling and join a support group.

I followed through on my promises and got involved in therapy. It has been a couple of years now and I sometimes get the urge to watch something pornographic, but those thoughts are quickly replaced with disdain for the entertainment which was destroying me and my marriage.

My marriage has gotten better in increments as my wife still needs time to heal and time to learn to trust me again. Anyone who thinks pornography viewing isn't detrimental, is in for a rude awakening if it gets out of hand!

Just how much porn viewing is too much? That's a good question! There is no right or wrong answer, nor is there an exact answer. Having stated the obvious, anyone who has ever had a porn addiction will tell you any amount of viewing, even a minute is bad, as it triggers the desire to watch more.

If you ask most people who watch porn why they watch it, they will tell you for entertainment/enjoyment. The porn serves nothing more than a catharsis, a stress release -- for some, we're guessing in more ways than one!

Everyone seeks something to provide them with some kind of enjoyment, stress release or pleasurable experience to help them escape the rigors of the outside world. Some even choose pornography to serve as their cathartic release---mental health escape. The question then becomes, why have they chosen porn? When this question is then followed up with the question, "Is the person watching porn married or in a relationship, then why do they feel the need to view porn secretly?" What is the main reason they watch porn and get hooked? Is it for:

1) Pure enjoyment?

2) Teach them things about improving their own sexual performance?

3) They are bored in their relationship and they fantasize about having sex with the women in the porn videos?

4) Sex with their spouse is not good?

5) In essence, they know their relationship is over and they don't care anymore?

If the first two reasons, it's the need to view porn for pure enjoyment or "educational" purposes, so then perhaps the relationship is not in trouble, or as much as in the other two situations. With that said, if a man is doing it for these first two reasons, then why is he doing it secretively, and why is he watching a lot of it? We're sure he would have further reasons to rationalize his irrationalizations.

When men watch a lot of porn because of reasons, #3, #4 and #5, then not only is their marriage/relationship in trouble, but they run the risk of becoming hooked on porn, that is if they are not already! Furthermore, the relationship they are in may be ending, but even if they were to jump into another relationship not long after, they have already conditioned themselves to become aroused in a certain manner. His next mate will have to measure up to that level of arousal. Even if she does in the beginning, sex in most relationships become common place after a while and usually need to be spiced up, but he has wired into his mind a means for a great way of arousing himself... Porn!

We've been discussing married men, or men in relationships who watch porn, but the same can hold true for single men who watch a lot of porn before getting into a committed relationship. They have habituated their minds/brains to a level of arousal correlated to viewing porn. Much like Pavlov's operant conditioning, or Bandura's Social Learning Theory , they develop a way of thinking in terms of sexual arousal. For those not familiar with Pavlov or Bandura, please check out any introductory psychology textbook or the Internet to find out how humans become conditioned and develop cognitive scripts -- the same patterns of thinking.

Did you know that some psychologist/researchers claim it takes only 21 days to form a habit, whether it be good or bad? Incidentally, once this habit is formed, it often takes a lot longer than 21 days to get rid of. The human brain becomes hard-wired to encode habits and new neural pathways are formed to transport these thought processes. Over time, these thoughts are entertained so often, that they become automatic, that the neural pathways kick in with just a thought, or a trigger... Perhaps viewing porn or thoughts of it in this instance.

What might have innocently or unintentionally started out as doing something for enjoyment may eventually turn into habit, or worse an addiction! Ask any alcoholic, drug addict or gambler who started out engaging in their vice "just for pleasure" how quickly it became an addiction. Most will tell you an addiction only needs a foothold to start out before it develops a stronghold over one's life.

An individual may have began their pornography viewing out of curiosity or catharsis. Over a period of time, the individual who becomes habituated to it, is most likely to develop a routine around porn viewing. Eventually, not only do they become habituated or even addicted to it, their sexual arousal is more likely to become dependent on porn. Individuals may need the porn to get aroused/satisfied, images/fantasies in their minds for gratification, or they may ask their partners to act out what they have seen in the porn flicks so they can achieve arousal.

When individuals engage in any vice for the purpose of arousal, gratification or to avoid pain, one of the major by-products becomes desensitization. When someone needs more of a "substance" through higher doses or greater frequencies, because they are not receiving the same degree of arousal they previously experienced, this is referred to as desensitization.

Desensitization is the hallmark of media because we are constantly bombarded with it on television, radio, news media and now Internet. Years ago what was once perceived as taboo in media and television is now seen as okay, or not bad because something stronger has come along and dethroned it as being more taboo or intolerable. Give the new intolerable media stuff some time and it will become "okay" or "not bad" because with repeated exposure to it, we grow use to it and accept it, even though we once thought it to be awful. And if that is not enough, something worse is on the horizon and when this comes along, what was once evil and/or bad is relatively good, compared to what's new in the media!

When it comes to viewing pornography, the same process occurs with repeated viewing experiences. Many viewers will start out with just minimal amounts of viewing. Before long it grows into prolonged periods -- hours! After they become less stimulated by what they are seeing, they seek out greater varieties. Finding what they are looking for in order to satiate their arousal becomes a challenge for many.

The interesting phenomenon for most married porn addicts is finding what is going to satisfy them at the expense of their relationship. For some, their wives merely "get in the way" of them finding what they need for sexual arousal.

Perhaps a great way to make this point is using the following amusement park analogy to compare porn to sexual relations with one's partner. Interestingly enough, those with porn addictions probably treat their bodies like their own private amusement park!

Say as a child your parents took you to a carnival where there were a variety of rides and games. For the next few years, you visited the carnival with your parents often. You had the time of your life as nothing compared to how much joy and fun the carnival provided for you. A couple of years later, your parents take you to Disney World. Words cannot describe how much excitement visiting Disney World provides you with. You thought you died and went to heaven!

When you get back home, months later your parents take you to the carnival because they know how much you like it. You look forward to it and when you finally get their you find yourself extremely bored... Disappointed! When your parents ask you if you are having fun, you tell them how much you want to go back to Disney World as well as the other theme parks you didn't yet see.

Okay, we know comparing carnivals/Disney to marriages/pornography probably isn't the most scientific comparison, but we think you get the point, especially if you have been to Disney World. Once you have had something which stimulates your senses to a level you have not yet experienced, you crave that experience again, or ones very similar to it. What you have already might satisfy you a little, but you constantly compare it to the "great" experience you just had or try to turn it into that. The problem is that it will not. And it can never match up to it.

Porn is an interesting monster in terms of sex addiction as well as the Madonna complex. It is available 24 hours a day, 7 days a week, in your own home, and if outside, in the palm of your own hand, no pun intended! We were referring to I-Pads and Blackberries.

Most addicts will tell you that one of precipitators which keeps their addictions going is instant gratification, or in this case, one's ability to delay it. Even when a married man with a porn addiction tries his best to stay away from porn and focus on his wife, cognitive scripts are burnt into his mind where he associates sex with arousal from porn, followed by auto-erotic stimulation. Of course some may even go further and require the experience using an actual female body.

If he is loyal to his wife, then a husband with a porn addiction and possessing Madonna complex is likely to start treating his wife like the actresses in the porn movies -- at least in the bedroom. He vicariously "uses" his wife to have sex with the women from the porn movies. He either treats his wife like a "whore" in the bedroom, or he has sex with her as he normally would while fantasizing about the women in the videos.

Some porn addicts possessing Madonna complex use strip clubs, massage parlours and escorts/prostitutes to satiate their sexual urges, hungers and fantasies. This is "okay" in their minds because they really are not cheating, rather using the services of a paid professional. Many would assert they are having a service provided to them and there is no feeling involved. "How does this possibly make this cheating on my wife?", they ask. We have interviewed some men who claim that this is pretty much the same as getting a real massage, the kind provided by a registered massage therapist. The only thing done differently they claim is they are getting "full body tension release".

The third possibility is for him to seek a mistress for sexual encounters. He prefers a mistress who will let him act out and/or role play his sexual fantasies. The only problem with this scenario is he and/or she, the mistress, are likely to develop feelings for one another over time. Also, since he is connected to someone non-professionally, then the likelihood of him getting caught is a lot higher. Porn on its own seems to be safer for married men in terms of not getting caught cheating. Ironically when they do cheat on their wives, they are most likely to use their wives to do the cheating by treating their wife like the desired porn star they fantasize about. When they do step out, it is usually with paid professionals to keep things safe and professional while minimizing their guilt and shame.

EVENING UP THE PLAYING FIELD - A CASE STUDY

I am a woman and proud of it! Some people perceive women as the weaker of the two sexes. I don't see it that way one bit. I want to throw something out there...

Submission! Think in terms of either domination and submission in the corporate world, real world or where it is often most interpreted -- sexual fetishes and role playing. I ask you, "Who is in control?"

Most think that the one holding all of the power is the dominant, especially in terms of sadomasochistic relationships. If that's what you think, then think again! Unless there is a sub, there is no master! Masters need slaves but do slaves really need masters? Think about that one! By the way, I have been into the lifestyle as a submissive for over a decade as well as being an educator so I know a little about how this tasty, ubiquitous relationship works.

I was asked the question, are women still considered the weaker of the two sexes in the real world and in the bedroom? I would have to say perceptions say yes, however reality says no! As a matter of fact, if you buy into the premise that women have always been the submissive of the two sexes, then that would mean they have always been the power holders.

Someone cannot have power unless they have someone to lead. And the one that allows them self to be led in essence holds all of the cards... They relinquish their freedoms and power.

As a matter of fact they control the circumstances that allow themselves to be controlled in the bedroom or in real life.

Do you get it? Women have always been the primary referent power holders!

Sexual liberation is stunning for both men and women. They violate the perception of being the weaker sex when all along they have been the more powerful based on their submission. Furthermore, when the "sub" starts acting dominant and becomes the "Dom" so to speak, they have done a 180 degree turn, rather they *have only added to their power! They get to be submissive and/or dominant in either situation and they possess all of the power!*

I think this dumbfounds some men, and some women because they are perceptive enough to see what is really going on... Women just got a dose of more power. When liberated women express themselves sexually, the reason they are perceived as "whores" or "bitches" is because they are a threat -- men jump to the beat of their drum! And I believe that those women who refer to other women this way, possess a sense of envy or jealousy because they didn't have the kutzpa to step out themselves!

The world we live in is and always will be about perceptions. Most perceptions are based on unchallenged stereotypes which are nothing more than short-cuts to these perceptions to begin with -- a circle which goes round and round. To finish off with my circle analogy, most have always believed the circle to be one of two things; a prison which has kept women within, when they have always wanted to get out, or a fortress for men which keeps women out, when they long to get in. Give me a break! The more I experience the world and people, the more I realize that women own the inner circle and everything outside it's perimeter.

They say "no man is an island", perhaps some men are closer to that reality than they think!

CHAPTER SUMMARY -- KEY POINTS

1) With heightened technological and media advancements, pornography is everywhere for viewers who choose to indulge in.

2) First off, sex sells today as it always has! If you go back to Freud's Life and Death Instinct theories back in the 1800's, you will see he was definitely on the money.

3) When men watch a lot of porn they run the risk of becoming hooked on porn.

4) Some psychologist/researchers claim it takes only 21 days to form a habit, whether it be good or bad!

5) Most sex addicts will tell you that one of precipitators which keeps their addictions going is instant gratification. Cognitive scripts are burnt into the mind where sex gets associated exclusively with arousal from porn.

CHAPTER SEVEN

**MADONNA
COMPLEX
ON THE INTERNET...**

CYBER SEX

Pornography is about dominance. Erotica is about mutuality.

Gloria Steinem

In previous chapters we discussed how the Internet has opened up a whole new world for experiencing sexuality -- pornography, chatting, role playing and cyber sex.

Where you have all of the aforementioned, you also have the propensity for infidelity and the Madonna complex on-line. Just how does the Madonna complex work via the Internet? It comes to life in one of two ways...

The Internet facilitates and makes available to men engaging in Madonna complex the ability to exploit women in one of two ways, or both; *Degradation and Infidelity*. Before we go any further we should point out that there are those who would assert that any woman participating on-line for the purpose of pornography or cyber sex is not really being exploited because they are willing participants in the Internet game of sex. That is very true and we do agree with this assertion to a point. Since we are referring to attached/married men in this book as the one's primarily possessing the Madonna complex, then the women being exploited are their wives and/or girlfriends. Coincidentally, we have even had women tell us who have been mistresses for married men that they felt like the ones being victimized -- cheated on! They could not see their role in the Madonna complex in that they were nothing more than sex objects and/or diversions for men from their married lives. Also, we should point out that wives who had been cheated on by these men, did not see their husbands' mistresses as victims. In fact, some of the wives has expressed to us that they wish they could see the mistress as "mud"!

When men believing in the aspects of the Madonna complex use the Internet for the degradation of women, they are doing so to carry out the negative perceptions they have of women while at the same time satisfying sexual/violent urges they may possess toward women.

Let's first start out by what we would define degradation to be. Degradation means to lower one's value or position in society, while bringing someone to a lower state through corruption or potential harm. Refer back to our early chapter on Misogyny. If you recall, misogyny is largely based on the hatred/loathing of women. A key component of misogyny is degradation brought about through the devaluing of women. There is little doubt this is often times created through sexual corruption and potential harm. If you do any research into the dominion of prostitution/sex trade, and speak with cops in "morality units", those branches of policing which track prostitution, they will tell you that the prostitute fits the description of a woman harmed/corrupted through degradation to a tee! The prostitute allows herself to become the slave of a pimp who mentally/emotionally/physically abuses/exploits her for money and often times controls her through beating her and getting her addicted to drugs; stimulants and barbiturates. When he isn't abusing her, then often times it is the "john", the man who uses her services. Peter has worked with police in morality units, as well as interviewed and professionally counselled sex trade workers and he has witnessed firsthand how this damaging and corruptive process works with sex trade workers.

The Internet has opened up a whole new way to degrade sex trade workers on-line or women in general who wish to engage in on-line cyber sex. For men, the best part is that if they are completely satisfied with getting their rocks off through cyber sex, then they can stretch the limits and degrade women to the infinite degree. Furthermore, they are able to protect their anonymity as well as their reputations.

Men who view women from a reference point of misogyny are obviously using them in an exploitive fashion -- a means to an end for sexual arousal/gratification. Since they view women as "sex objects" and less than men, then these women serve as their "toys", to be used in their fantasies and role plays on the internet. For those men who are sexually deviant (possessing paraphilias such as sadism, fetishes, voyeurism and exhibitionism -- refer to Diagnostic and Statistical Manual) and hold a strong hatred towards women, they are more likely to want fantastical role plays to be based on sexual violence -- assaults, forced rapes, humiliation, demeaning and degradation. Peter lectures on courses in criminal psychology and sexual violence and points to research the FBI in the USA as well as other police services around the world have done on sexual deviants. "Most of what experts find on sexual deviants and sadistic rapists is the perception of misogyny in women," states Peter.

Even though the study of sexual deviants is disturbing, yet interesting, this book will only stick to men using the Internet for cyber sex and role playing fantasies. These men possess misogyny, yet they are able to keep it controlled whereby they don't feel the need to act it out in the real world with an unwilling victim!

TOM'S CASE STUDY

I agreed to speak about this in strict confidence and I gave permission to use my story on the agreement that my real name would be changed.

I used to spend a lot of time on the internet role playing. I was a married man at the time and I am still married to the same woman now for almost 12 years. I am also a sex addict in recovery. I spent thousands of dollars on telephone chat lines over ten years ago where I would role play either in my head or on the phone with the women I would chat with. I was dating my wife to be at the time and then married her while still engaging in this secret life.

First let me say that my wife is one of the classiest women you could ever meet. Seriously, why she is with me is a mystery! I love her and wouldn't do anything to purposely hurt her or my daughter. I was just so intrigued and hooked on screwing around on the telephone and then eventually the Internet. There were really bad, taboo things I wanted to do to women. I fantasized about violent acts of sex. I agreed I would not be too descriptive here in discussing what I did and I also wish to forget about it at this point for two reasons, one, it is degrading to all women as well as myself as a human and second, I don't want it to trigger any arousing feelings!

I never really wanted to just have straight sex with women -- just screw! I wanted vicious, wild sex with women. For whatever reason I never had a lot of respect for women. I don't see them as my equal. I think much of that has to do with the way I was raised and seeing my father abuse my own mother when I was young. As I got older the abuse stopped as my father got helped and my parents for the most part appeared happy. What I saw stuck with me. What I used to choose to watch on TV had women being abused by men. The pornography I enjoyed watching most had women being submissive and being abused by men. It really turned me on!

Don't get me wrong, I am not a serial killer or rapist or anything like that. The thought of hurting a woman that bad never crossed my mind. The thought of her fighting me though was a major turn on. Did I ever suggest this to my wife or ask her to do this? Hell no! I wouldn't go there with her. As I said, I have too much respect for her and would worry she would leave me if she heard me utter these suggestions.

As for the telephone chat lines where you can meet people locally to chat with or meet up with, that really set the ball rolling for me. I was spending as much as four sometimes eight hours a day on the phone. You see, at first it was free. Then after about a year, you had to pay for it. I guess they knew you could get hooked on it and come back for more. That was me!

In the first year and a half I didn't meet anyone. I mostly role played taboo sex on the telephone with women, at least those who would oblige. Eventually, I needed to meet women. For the next two years I sort of became a stalker. I would set up meeting women and then show up but not approach them. I would hide and study them from a distance, sometimes using binoculars. I was finding having visuals to go with the conversations. I will admit that most of the women were nothing like they described themselves to be physically. In fact, many were really overweight. This made it easier to not cross the line and attempt to have real sexual relations with them and cheat on my soon-to-be-wife. I know if I would have cheated it would have eaten me away inside. So I played this game for a long while. At the same time my phone bills started to accumulate into the hundreds, sometimes thousands of dollars. It had totally grown out of control!

Eventually I found free sites on the Internet to use. This was like winning the lottery! I could see photos of women, chat on-line and have lower phone bills as I was still addicted to the phone chat lines. Ironically, I used the Internet to wean myself off of the telephone!

In time I was really getting hooked on the Internet and playing on it, we were using dial-up modem. This kept things slow or the computer would freeze up. This caused me a lot of rage and frustration. I felt like a junkie unable to get his full fix. Hence this is still why I had a preference for phone chat lines.

Eventually I would get more into porn sites on-line. This made streaming of video easier. I was also able to find on-line chat girls -- pay for play who engage you in whatever fantasies you want. When live cams came along, this was like a cocaine addict having the purest form of coke dropped into their lap. I became a vicious junkie!

At the time this was really getting bad in my life, our daughter was born. During the first couple of years of my daughter's life, it was easier to engage in my on-line sex addictions as my wife was very busy with our daughter. I also got into meeting up with women publicly in parks or parking lots and just chatting. It was getting to the point where I was going to have an affair in a hotel room or drive out of town to a woman's home. I was looking for women on-line who advertised they were submissive and seeking a master to abuse them. I was just two weeks away from having my first real encounter with a woman I had been chatting with on-line for a couple of months who lived a couple of hours away from me. She had no idea I was married. My wife had no idea about this woman either, until one night when she found a picture of the woman I had printed off the computer. The printer had frozen earlier in the day and printed duplicates. I took the one picture I thought it had printed not seeing the other in the tray. My wife found it and later questioned me. I down-played it and was eventually able to wiggle my way out of it. This did not come without intense suspicion on my wife's part though. She knew I was up to something, but she didn't know quite what it was.

I chose not to meet the woman to have the affair with, and I cut all communication off with her immediately. I deleted myself from every website I was on where I had profiles. I thought I did a great job of covering everything up. I didn't!

I paid all of the bills and my wife never saw a phone bill or credit card bill. But when she went looking, she found them. She saw all of my 1-900 phones calls as well as my payments via the credit card to the porn sites on-line. She waited to address the issue when I got home from work that day. I was totally busted! There *was no way of lying my way out of this as the evidence was right in front of me. She also was able to see some of the websites I had visited. She also asked me to open up my e-mail accounts for her to see. I told her I wouldn't. Instead I told her about my addictions to pornography and the Internet websites for chatting. I never had an affair so I told her the truth in that regard, that I had never cheated even though I had thoughts about it. I did tell her that much. I didn't dare tell her about the sexual fantasies and role plays I was having with hundreds of women. I led her to believe there had been only a couple of women over the last couple of years... I never mentioned this was going on for a decade. I know this much... I love my wife and couldn't live without her! I also knew at the time I was relieved in some twisted way that she found out so this might be the push/threat I needed to quit this humiliating and expensive addiction I was into. Telling her the complete history and story of my antics would only make things worse and unfixable. I was ready to quit and get help so I logically thought no more wrongs would make this situation any better. And to this day that was as much as she was ever told even though a part of me had and still has some guilt today. Why should I make her more upset than she already was? Why should I hurt my daughter as well? I never really cheated so why talk about something that could have been? You might think of me as a liar and coward but I was trying to hold onto whatever dignity I had left as well as my family!*

I admitted to my wife I had a sex addiction to pornography and dirty sex. This was the truth. What bothered her most I think is that I didn't engage in any of these "dirty sex" fantasies with her. She reassured me that she would have been open to them... Possibly! How do you tell your wife you have rape/assault fantasies? How do you tell the woman you most adore in the world that you have a great disdain for women? Needless to say I never told her how bad these fantasies really were or what they are about!

To this day I am a member of a support group dealing with sex addictions. Even though I have come a long way, I still get tempted to see what's out there and on-line. In the last couple of years, technology has made it even more tempting!

The case of Tom provides some insight into why men use the Internet, from a misogyny frame of reference. The other side of the coin has men using the Internet as an alternative for actually cheating. Many engage in fantasies on-line with complete strangers because they know these women will always truly be strangers to them and that they will not step out of their marriages and cheat on their wives.

Some time ago we polled both college students as well as people on the streets by asking them one simple question: If you are in a relationship and you go on-line and have cyber sex or just talk about sex with others, have you cheated on your mate? Did you know that nearly 20% of the people we asked believed that having cyber sex with someone you don't know even though you have a mate is not really cheating? Wow! The majority of those making up the 20%, of those claiming it was okay, were men. Of course we had to follow up the big question with a chain of smaller ones to see what they were thinking. We asked questions like;

1) Why don't you consider it cheating?
2) Is it only cheating when you have physical contact with someone?
3) If it's not cheating, then do you tell your mate that you are doing it?
4) Do you feel guilty about doing it?

5) If it's not cheating, then would you care if your mate came to you and
said they were doing it is as well?

6) Why do you feel the need to engage in cyber sex with strangers?

And this is where the answers become somewhat redundant... Even hairy!

When asked the first question, those that didn't consider it cheating asserted there was no real sex! Some believed it is the same as masturbation or using porn to enhance their autoerotic pleasure.

In terms of the second question, those who did not believe cyber sex is cheating claimed it is only cheating if there is real sex, i.e. intercourse and/or oral sex. Furthermore, many also believed if you only kissed someone (necking) that this wasn't cheating either. Some even believed that "touching" someone in the privates wasn't cheating!

Those who didn't tell their mates they were doing it, believed it wasn't their mate's business. Just as they don't tell their mate they are masturbating, they don't discuss their cyber experiences either, since they believe it is their business alone and they are doing no wrong. "Why start an argument where one doesn't have to exist?" some asserted.

Those who stated they didn't feel guilty over having cyber sex claimed they felt the same way as they would if they were engaging in masturbation. It's all about fantasy and role playing in their minds. In fact, they felt they could go to women on-line, express their fantasies and fetishes and not be rejected.

Of the nearly 20% of the men who claimed it was all right for them to do it, some stated they would be offended if their mates were engaging in cyber-sex with other guys. In this case it was more based on ego. They felt that if their mates are looking elsewhere, then this man must not be "good enough" in the bedroom. Interestingly, these men believed that women for the most part prefer "regular", vanilla sex, whereas men by their nature are more perverse and prefer wild sex. Some believed that by having cyber-sex and not asking his mate to perform certain acts, he was actually maintaining each of their dignities!

Finally, when asked about the need to engage in cyber-sex with strangers, the answer was simple... Variety! Once again holding to the integrity and virtue theme, attached men who believed cyber-sex was okay for them, claimed it allowed them to vent and/or act out sexual urges that may offend, "gross out" or anger their partner. Since they were doing it with complete strangers and anonymously, this removed all stigma of it being real sex. As one put it, "If it's faceless, then it's sexless... Not real!"

On a more humorous note, we asked, "What if the supposed woman you are having cyber-sex was really a man pretending to be a woman?" Most were initially and immediately grossed out and some very defensive claiming, "I'm not gay!". With that said, they quickly same back with the concept of "perception". Since it is on the computer and you perceive the other person to be a woman to help live out a fantasy, at the end of the day it really doesn't matter who is on the other end of the computer since you already have the naughty fantasy rehearsed in your head and you already know how you want the other person to look like, regardless!

KATE'S COMPETITOR - A CASE STUDY

I had problems in my marriage for many years. We finally split up a couple of years ago. I always worried about and wondered if my husband was cheating on me. As it turned out, he was and he wasn't. And that depends on whether you are asking him or me!

My husband was big time into porn both in terms of movies and on the Internet. He really got into the live web porn sites. He was dropping hundreds of dollars playing around on them. Yes, I was aware of it!

Before we got married and even after, we were into watching porn. He was into it more than I was, but it would turn me on to see him aroused. Also, I was happy he was using porn at home instead of hanging out in the strip clubs or picking up women and doing them without me knowing. We had a pretty open marriage in terms of sexual liberties -- watching porn, role playing and we even tried threesomes a while back. It was the threesome that first showed me how my man could behave with a woman that was not me. I found him utterly aggressive and intrusive to the woman we were with. It was after that encounter that I drew the line there would be no more threesomes whatsoever. I saw a different man during that encounter and also after viewing porn. Anyone who believes watching porn is completely harmless, think again... You're delusional! It is one way to wreck a marriage, namely my own.

When he watched porn he got into more aggressive versions of it, especially on the Internet. When I used to question him on it, he would really lose it on me and blow up! I left him to his porn. One thing I noticed though is that our physical intimacy dropped off. I discussed why he wasn't into me as much anymore and what I could do to make things better. It was when he suggested that we do our own porn on the Internet that things fell apart. He found a site where you could tape yourself or go live and people would pay to watch. It was the stupidest thing I ever heard of. Needless to say I said no! That didn't stop him. Behind my back he started doing it alone on the Internet. Men and women would actually pay to watch him. He would also continue to watch them and get off. I had enough of it all and confronted him with the notion that he was in essence cheating on me. He thought it was insane and didn't believe that he was being unfaithful. When he saw me so pissed off, he promised to stop. I thought he did.

It was months later that someone I know saw him on-line still doing who knows what! I never even confronted him on the matter. I left him and moved in with a best friend while I filed for divorce. He didn't fight me nor contest the divorce. At the end of the day, he claimed he did nothing wrong and that porn was nothing more than recreational. This whole thing for him as he put it, was a "pleasant diversion"!

CHAPTER SUMMARY - KEY POINTS

1) When men believing in the aspects of the Madonna complex use the Internet for the degradation of women, they are doing so to carry out the negative perceptions they have of women while at the same time satisfying sexual/violent urges they may possess toward women.

2) Internet cyber sex and role playing fantasies allow misogyny to occur where men can control themselves privately, whereby they don't feel the need to act it out in the real world!

3) Attached men who believe cyber-sex is okay claim that it allows them to vent and/or act out sexual urges that may offend, "gross out" or anger their partners.

CHAPTER EIGHT

INFIDELITY

The natural man has only two primal passions, to get and beget.

William Osler

In chapter 6 we briefly touched upon how someone with a porn addiction and possessing the Madonna complex could be inclined to step out of their marriage/relationship in order to quench their carnal appetites. In this chapter we will move full-speed in discussing the how's, what's, whys, when's and even where's individuals with Madonna complex engage in, to experience instant gratification/satisfaction in this area of their lives. Unfortunately these individuals are selfish fulfilling their needs while hurting others who love them most!

To begin, it is best to discuss/describe what one's perception of cheating is. If you remember at the beginning of this book we asked you to ponder through a list of questions. This was to establish what sorts of values you hold toward marriage and relationships overall. With that said, what do you consider cheating to entail? Everyone's perception of what cheating really is, differs. Remember, some men believe that if they use the services of a paid professional (escort/prostitute) then it is not cheating because it is emotionless and they are paying someone to provide them with a professional service.

Too many live with the notion today that "if it feels good, then do it!" The problem is sometimes what feels good for one has the ability to hurt another -- a spouse who has been cheated on. One may have enjoyed their fling and now needs forgiveness, while the other is in a perpetual state of surviving infidelity!

What is cheating? Actual sex/intercourse? Or does it include any oral sex, petting/touching, kissing, talking about it, even Internet cyber sex without any intercourse? Often times the one committing infidelity has a much different perception from the victim of what infidelity is!

Why are rates of infidelity so high these days? Technology and media have made cheating easier as individuals have Internet and Blackberries. Did you know that some stats show as many as 35% of women cheat or have cheated on their spouses? Furthermore, estimates show that 7 out of 10 men have acted outside of their marriages/relationships. Of course most of infidelity stats are not the by-product of the Madonna complex, but some are!

TONY'S EXCUSE - A CASE STUDY

Do I believe one can cheat on their spouse and it be okay? Absolutely! Before judging me a pig, at least hear me out!

I have been married for ten years. Before we got married and right after, sex was amazing. We did it often and it was an absolute kick. As our careers became busier and then when we had our daughter, things started to change.

First of all, I found that the sex wasn't as interesting and wild as it once was. When my wife got pregnant, she wanted to still have sex, but I didn't. As she got bigger, I worried about hurting the baby as well as found it kind of strange to have sex with a pregnant woman. At one point because of the size of the baby, she really couldn't have sex. She still wanted to satisfy me. Something inside of me clicked and made me feel that it was just wrong. She wasn't just my wife anymore, she was also the mother of my daughter. For the last two months of her pregnancy, I decided to take matters into my own hands. She was aware of it and was actually okay with it. She felt bad that she couldn't have sex and felt that she was letting me down.

When the baby came along things really changed. I was in the delivery room for the birth and what I saw sort of initially put me off having sex with my wife. If you have ever witnessed a birth, it is the most beautiful thing in the world. Also, if you have only seen your spouse in a sexual light rather than a baby-maker, it has the ability to gross you out... And it did!

As my wife was getting larger during pregnancy so were her breasts. During the first few months it was a major turn on for me. What guy doesn't like bigger breasts on a woman right? After she gave birth, they were still big as she was breast feeding our daughter. It didn't take me long to watch my daughter breast feeding as well as see the breast milk, for me to know those breasts were off-limits for me! It wasn't my wife who posed this rule on me, rather I self-imposed it. I just could not see myself sharing the same breasts that my daughter was feeding from.. Some guys find it sexy or kinky to drink their wife's breast milk, but I found it sickening to think about it. My wife once joked about that I could have the leftovers later that night. For whatever reason, that only added to my aversion of her sexually.

In the next couple of years, we rarely had sex. My wife was usually busy with our daughter as well as running her business from our house. We managed to get pregnant again within the next two years as we both wanted another child and we wanted our daughter to have a sibling. After my son was born, there was basically no more sex. She still wanted to, but not as much. I never really wanted to at all. This would lead me to stepping out in my marriage and eventually getting caught by my wife!

One of the things I liked most about sex was foreplay, namely oral sex. I loved to receive as well as give. After seeing the birth of my daughter, there was no way I could ever go down on my wife again. The thought of it made me gag. The last thing I wanted to do was gag and puke while I was pleasing her. You get the point! I really liked receiving oral sex a lot actually. My wife still did it for me with less frequency during the first *pregnancy. After watching her kiss my daughter as a baby, there was no way I was going to let her go down on me again. There was something totally not right with that picture! We did try it a few times, but I found I could not climax, or better yet, I fought the urge too. I literally talked myself out of having an orgasm!*

Within a year, I found myself almost totally impotent around my wife. When I was alone, taking care of myself, I didn't have that problem, well at least not as often. I did find that I was bordering on having impotence. I think it was more psychological than anything. When I took some natural supplements to stimulate erections, they seemed to work. My wife thought I had a problem with impotence and I think she didn't push me into sex with her because she thought I felt bad that I couldn't perform. Whatever way you look at it, our sex life became a complete wash. And I was completely happy with that!

It was about that time I started going to strip clubs alone. There are some locally, but I chose to drive out of town and go to the clubs which were nearly a half hour away. At first I would just watch. Eventually I would go to the VIP rooms with the girls and receive hand jobs. Eventually it became oral sex.

I didn't think I was cheating on my wife since she wasn't doing this for me and I wouldn't let her. I wasn't even worried about getting caught at this point. What worried me most was contracting a sexually transmitted disease. I was always insistent on wearing a condom. If those girls were willing to do me, I am sure they were doing everyone and his brother!

The only type of sex I would have with the girls at the clubs was either hand jobs or oral sex, so more them doing me. Since I never got this at home, I never saw it as cheating. To go one step further, I really looked at it as a type of massage. For me, cheating would be going all the way and having sex. That is something that is saved for someone you love because it is more meaningful. I do those kinds of thing with my wife. With sex, a woman can become pregnant and before you know it, you are a father. That is cheating in my books as well as giving oral to a woman. I would view both situations as too personal! There are a lot of women who find going down on a man dirty. Also, I think that to ask for oral sex from my wife or expect it, may put her in an uncomfortable situation. it makes me feel bad for asking and in some ways it makes me feel like I am treating her like a cheap thrill!

I didn't view what I was doing as cheating, or at least completely cheating on my wife. I was paying a woman to satisfy me and do a service for me. My wife didn't think the same way I did.

A client of my wife's business saw me a couple of times at the club. He let it slip out during one of their meetings. She confronted me with me denying it at first before finally giving in. The argument lasted for days. She would not speak to me unless I was going to be completely honest with her. My wife knew when I was lying or whenever I was withholding the truth from her. She caught me in a web of lies and deceit. I fought with myself as to whether or not to come completely clean. Finally, I thought it would be best if I told her everything I did with the girls at the club. I sincerely explained my reasons for doing what I did. Initially my wife was stunned. She wasn't as stunned about me doing things with the girls, as much as she was over how I viewed her basically as a sexless woman... A mother only. This created a lot of turmoil in our marriage and family for months to come.

It took a long while to get forgiveness from her. Not once did she bring up the word divorce. If she would have divorced me I don't know what I would have done. I felt horrible over what I had done not only for the hurt I caused her but also for the place I put my kids in. I agreed to see a counsellor and I also joined a support group. It was a help. They could help me work on myself and my thought process but they could not help me fix the damage I had done to my wife's ego.

It has now been a couple of years since the, you know what, hit the fan and I still belong to some men's groups. I can't say our marriage is back to normal, nor can I say it has gotten better. It has become different. We have more communication in our marriage and we have tried to work on our intimacy which is coming along slowly. The biggest obstacle I now face in my marriage is trust, that is receiving my wife's trust unconditionally. At first I worried about whether or not I could trust myself. The counselling has helped as well as accepting what I have done and forgiving myself. I love my wife a lot and one of the things I have learned is not to act on feelings, rather think things through. Feelings can really wreck things because they are usually irrational and not grounded in realities. The overall reality is I was living a lie, believing a lie and deceiving people including myself.

There is the old media adage, "What happens in Vegas, stays in Vegas!" This translated can best been interpreted as, "What you don't know won't hurt you!" Unfortunately, this is the belief fallacy too many individuals committing infidelity cling onto. What they fail to realize is that the one they are hurting besides their mate is themselves. Lies will catch up, the facades and illusions will become more transparent, and trying to keep up fronts will become more work than living a simple everyday life.

Peter is author of the non-fiction book *Fast Food Dating Your 2 Cents* which explored dating services and venues available for people to use to find their dating matches. One of the chapters in the book was devoted to Internet dating and the best sites to meet people. A very precarious Internet site was one created for married people who wanted to cheat on their spouses. "I was totally blown away after I conducted my interview with one of the head PR people for this dating site, " Peter recalls. "It was a site that helps, encourages and even condones cheating on spouses and interestingly, the message is it's good to experience -- variety is the spice of life!"

If you study the media long and deep enough, you will find that in many circles the underlying message is that it is okay to cheat -- everybody is doing it! Too many people accept infidelity as a societal norm. Centuries ago, even decades ago, infidelity was primarily reserved for married men to engage in. Today, married women are also participants in oceans of infidelity. Why?

The Madonna complex is a major precipitator in today's generation. We are not saying that the Madonna complex is the cause of all or even most of cheating, but it is the cause in some cases and have a very interesting influence.

For men, the Madonna complex encourages men to cheat for the original reasons as described in earlier chapters in the book as well as retaliation to women who engage in cheating based on reversed Madonna complex. At this point you might be scratching your head asking, "What the heck is reversed Madonna complex?" Glad you asked!

Reversed Madonna complex is the sexual liberation of women who are now turning the tables and doing back to men what was once done to them. Back in the day, it was almost expected that some men would cheat and that it was "okay". Most women would take their cheating spouses back. Conversely, when women cheated on their men, it was not okay and men were less likely to take their wives back. Husbands perceived their wives as used/damaged goods (dirty) and some became psychologically distraught -- they wondered and worried if they could "measure up" to the man their wives had flings with. Rather than risk further humiliation and psychological contempt, it was easier to suffer loneliness and lack of forgiveness than to risk further rejection. Also, in some countries cheating wives were stoned to death!

Women were more likely to take back their cheating husbands because they knew that often the "fling" they were having was nothing more than just that... A fling, devoid of emotion and love. It was simply "just sex"! Their husbands were acting out reasons based on Madonna complex. Implied message: It was either expected of them and/or, they couldn't help themselves.

Interestingly, if you were to apply the same Madonna complex for cheating wives, it wouldn't hold the same water. Cheating women would be seen as doing what they are doing more so out of premeditation. They would be viewed as; sluts, bitches and whores for cheating on their husbands. Neo-feminists might contend this is part of being a liberated woman, to take and do things for herself because it feels good. Just as there is affirmative action in the workplace and careers, there could also be in terms of sexual attitudes and values. Men have been doing it for centuries and if all men (women) are truly created equally, then why can't wives cheat on their husbands and be granted the same lee-way? Why can't they be "studs", "macho", "drive by their homes", or "just men being men (women being women in this case)"? Simply, society does not or will not cater and condone to women cheating the same way that it does to men. In fact, they can be single and screw around with different partners and still be considered all of the above derogatory names and then some. It may appear that the playing field has become levels in many ways today for men and women, however it would appear that perceptions are still sloped toward favouring men.

To close this chapter, we decided to include a case study featuring Ronnie's story. We spoke with her and Ronnie discussed how frustrated she was with her husband and even began believing the worst -- he was cheating on her! Sometimes when we are over-emotional, we think the worst of people and ourselves. This often leads us to do things or act out desperately as Ronnie did.

BEING A VICTIM OF A SEXLESS MARRIAGE - RONNIE'S CASE STUDY

I was in a sexless marriage for two years. Matt and I have been married for four years. In the beginning there was lots of sex in our marriage. As a matter of fact, most of the best sex came before we were married. In the second year into our marriage, I found that I was the one always having to initiate sex with my husband, even force him into having sex with me. Matt would have sex with me, but it was always at the expense of a complaint -- something hurt, he was too tired, he didn't feel good, etc. Watching TV and reading books you would think he was using all of the excuses women traditionally use to get out of sexual relations with men! But my Matty was using everything under the sun to avoid having sex with me!

This really started to affect me mentally, emotionally which in turn made me feel physically ill. I really started to think there was something seriously wrong with me. I wondered if I had suddenly become so unattractive to him. I used to ask him things like, "Do you still find me attractive?", "Don't you enjoy having sex with me?", "Is there something I am doing wrong in the bedroom?" And each time he would reassure me that everything was okay and that it was him and work, and not me! Well, there must be something wrong with me... Without sex, it felt more like a coexistence rather than a relationship. Whoever heard of a sexless marriage when a couple is young and pretty much still newlyweds?

I met with my best friend one afternoon and remember telling her what was going on with Matt. I was so embarrassed to discuss my sexless marriage but needed to get it out. She was dumbfounded as she thought we had the perfect marriage and all was well behind closed doors. Not the case she soon realized!

I was quite hesitant to bring up my situation because I worried what she might toss out at me -- Matt is probably cheating... Getting it from somewhere else! This topic of conversation did arise and it made perfect sense. A man who was as sexually aggressive and passionate as Matt just doesn't up and quit is sexual urges overnight. I was too naive to assume it, let alone believe it. Sure enough all of the signs pointed toward Matt having an affair. It was during my conversation with my friend that the idea of me having an affair came up. The idea had never popped into my mind before, however when it did, it came in like gang-busters and wouldn't leave. Fast-forward two months later...

There was still no sex in my marriage. My husband's ability to perform was still M.I.A. At this point the idea of stepping out and having an affair appealed to me more and more as the days passed. I found myself hooked on Internet chat rooms and dating sites. It was all supposed to start out and remain innocent. Before long I was into cyber sex. Not long after that, I was a cyber whore! I was suddenly doing many men with my fingertips -- keyboard of course!

As much as I knew it was very wrong, I continued to enjoy it and endured the guilt thereafter. When Matt would come home I would literally despise him even more, for not having sex with me and making me feel like I had to do something to prove myself worthy as a woman. And then there was the affair! I was *so sure he was screwing around but I still hadn't confronted him on it. And then finally, I did it!*

I went out into the real world to meet a man from the Internet I had been having cyber sex with to have real sex with. We met discreetly in a town close by for drinks. We would get a hotel room close-by and go for it. All went smoothly so to speak, up until the hotel room experience. My heart raced the entire time leading up to it. He was handsome, had a great body and was just sexy! I couldn't wait to jump him. And then reality set in...

We drove in our separate vehicles to the hotel. He was in the lead. Sensing we were almost there, rationale and morality set in. I opted for the chicken door and spun off down a side street. I couldn't do it. No matter how you cut it, it was wrong. I was a married woman!

I was so angry with myself for being moralistic. I was even more peeved at Matt for screwing around on me! It was time to confront him...

That night I told him what had almost happened and why it had gotten to that point. He was filled with mixed emotions. He was visibly upset. It didn't take him long to break down and confess to the "one time" encounter he had. Without getting into the gory details, he stepped out on me once and once only. He couldn't have sex with me because of the guilt he felt. He believed I would "feel that woman" on him. He also worried he might have contracted an STD or something and didn't want me to catch it. He had been checked out and was clean, other than the guilt which polluted his conscience.

We discussed our situation and what we would do to salvage our marriage. It has been a few years now and things have somewhat gone back to normal. I still have trust issues, but I have to expect the best from the man I married rather than worrying about what he might be doing.

We have since had a little boy and I am looking to having a second child in the next couple of years. Matt has been a great husband and even better father since the troubles and confrontation.

I have forgiven him for stepping out of our bind of trust. I don't think I could have forgiven myself as easily or ever, if I would have stepped out. I think this stems from how I was raised and how society looks at women and expects them to behave.

CHAPTER SUMMARY -- KEY POINTS

1) Some men believe that if they use the services of a paid professional (escort/prostitute) then it is not cheating because it is emotionless and they are paying someone to provide them with a professional service.

2) Technology and media have made cheating easier as individuals have Internet and Blackberries. Some estimates show that 7 out of 10 men have acted outside of their marriages/relationships.

3) The Madonna complex encourages men to cheat as retaliation to women who engage in cheating, based on reversed Madonna complex.

4) Reversed Madonna complex is the sexual liberation of women who are now turning the tables and doing back to men what was once done to them.

CHAPTER NINE

SEX

ADDICTION

People spend a lifetime searching for happiness; looking for peace. They chase idle dreams, addictions, religions, even other people, hoping to fill the emptiness that plagues them. The irony is the only place they ever needed to search was within.

Ramona L. Anderson

Whenever discussing addiction, there is always great debate over what is a habit and what is an addiction. Sometimes, the notion of "choice" comes into the discussion with people disgruntled toward addicts accusing them of choosing their addiction or the sets of behaviours leading to the addiction. In today's media, when celebrities get caught with their hands in cookie jars (cheating -- no pun intended to cookies!) they often time claim they have a "sex addiction". Is there really such thing as a sex addiction?

Though there is much debate on the concept of sex addiction, we believe that it is a real issue. Generally the term is defined as a psychological condition where the individual (male or female) has an inability to manage their sexual behaviour. Often times the condition is looked at through the same lens of substance abuse as well as control issues within the individual.

Before we move on further in this chapter and explain sex addiction and whether it is real or not, let's first discuss what an addiction is. Peter has been a professor in psychology and has taught in an addiction studies program for 12 years, while writing this book. He has had the great fortune of working with addicts in recovery, working with leading treatment centers as well as getting first hand research on what is going on in the world of addiction. The starting point in determining whether or not sex can be an addiction, or anything for that matter is to determine the criterion and what necessitates an addiction. For the purpose of this book, we will define an addiction according to the following criteria:

Addiction is an uncontrollable compulsion to engage in repetitiously the same behaviour regardless of the negative consequences which occur because of that behaviour.

It is important to point out that even though the concept of "addiction" carries in it certain stereotypes and relegations, no two addictions are the same! The criterion for addictions include any and all of the following:

1) Addictions do not discriminate!

2) Addiction is a progressive and insidious disease which happens over time.

3) The user/addict develops a tolerance for the substance, whether it be psychological, physiological, or both.

4) Individuals experience withdrawal symptoms as soon as they try to stop using. These might be either physiological or psychological.

5) Individuals have tried repeated times to quit on their own or with the help of others and can't. Thinking you can do it alone is magical thinking!

6) Individuals will traverse through psychological stages before, during and after treatment and recovery. (Moods and behavior run the entire gambit of emotions.)

7) Relapse is often times a part of the recovery process.

8) Some individuals use substances because it provides   them   a means of instant gratification or a quick fix.

9) Some individuals become psychologically conditioned to use due to environment, social factors or triggers which stimulate the use followed by the user's response.

10) Some individuals engage in substance use to alleviate emotional or physical pain and enjoy the rapid numbing relief the drug provides.

11) The availability or easy access of the substance creates a stimulus to use the drug.

12) Being healed or cured is part of the recovery process. Only one in recovery can determine and acknowledge when they are truly healed or cured .

---

* Certain people are more prone to develop addictions than other people. This hinders their ability to find fulfillment, whether or not they actually develop specific addictions.

This is the best way to define and incorporate the qualities of an addiction. To move forward in our discussion in terms of sex being an addiction, one would have to examine the aforementioned criterion and see if another's or their own sexual behaviours fits within the standards that would define sex as an addiction.

Sex addiction and sexual compulsivity are one and the same. As a matter of fact, sexual compulsivity is a more modern, and in many cases a more politically correct way of saying sex addiction. Most theorists and therapists use the term sexual compulsivity. One of the primary factors affecting a person who possesses a compulsion towards sex is their fear of intimacy. One can clearly see how sexual compulsivity can be connected just through this in and of itself. People with addictive personalities have difficult times sustaining relationships. Addicts, prefer the immediate pleasurable sensation and tend to hide from relationships.

Anything that numbs the pain (emotional or physical) can become compulsive. In the case of sex, they turn to it as a way of distracting themselves from their problems. They believe that if they ignore their problems, they might magically go away.

In the case of the Madonna complex the male usually becomes compulsive with women (whores) as a way to deal with his pain from the relationship he has/had with his mother. These men see women as only good or bad -- Madonna's or whores. After he has sex with the "whore" once or many times, eventually he has to move on to the next woman because he cannot be deeply intimate with the women he has sex with. He then begins to jump from woman to woman trying to avoid the emotional anguish within. He learns to manipulate women to get what he wants. It is not uncommon for him to say flattering things which he doesn't believe in order for a woman to have sex with him. After they have conquered this type of woman, "the whore", he chucks her to the side of the road. She has served her purpose to him.

Any type of affairs this man engages in, is generally perceived as escaping commitment even if he is already married or in a serious relationship. He knows in advance that he could never commit to a whore. So through his intense mask of romancing (sexing) the "whore", he feels momentarily free, single and completely in touch with his machismo self. In fact, he might even get caught up in the passion or the connection his "whore" feels and feed into it momentarily. Eventually he comes to his senses and knows it can't nor will it last. Once the pseudo-passion has worn off, which could be anywhere from one night onward, he is ready to move on to his next "victim"!

Some theorists look at this as a split in the personality stemming from the relationship to his mother. One side of the personality does whatever the mother wants him to do as a child growing up. This side of his personality allows him to form some type of connection to his mother and feels as though he is pleasing her. Conversely, the other side develops a sense of narcissism and righteousness -- entitlement to possess and do what he wants to do. This is the intense side of his persona, the aspect which constantly needs to be fed and satiated.

The persona houses the elements which foster the addictive personality part of him. This is the part of him which nourishes the "sex addict" inside of him.

Most addicts are liars and great manipulators. They lie to and take advantage of others. There is a side of them that learns how to be, say and do the things which will get them what they want. This same side aids them in feeling little or no remorse for what they are doing even though they know it is wrong. Sex addicts operate from the same premise. He too evolves into intense "lover" and manipulator. Ironically, his wife rarely if ever, gets glimpses of this "lover" side of him. This is saved for the "dirty girls", the ones he perceives as the types who are easily disposable. And the more he matures, he learns to separate two distinct personalities; *Good Boy* and *Bad Boy*. The good boy is saved for his wife, kids, family, friends, colleagues, etc., while the bad boy is saved for his secret life -- the dark side no one knows about, other than his mistresses.

BRIAN'S STORY - A CASE STUDY

Brian was a 45 year old male who never married. He had been in one long term relationship from age 30 to about age 35. He recalls that after the first 6 months his desire for his girlfriend started to decrease. He disclosed that they waited about 6 months to have sex and had sex a few times a week for the next six months. Brian does not know why to this day he stopped desiring his girlfriend as he stated the relationship was great. He stated that he felt they were pretty good friends having the occasional argument. He stated that after the second year together she started going out with her friends more, but he also stated that the sex issues started the year before. As the relationship progressed, they were having sex on average once every 6 months and it seemed to be a struggle on his part!

Brian stated that his sex drive was pretty much the same. In fact, he was even more sexually aroused by other women. Brian admitted that he would go down to the strip club in the city a couple times a week and pay for lap dances and "other" activities. He also admitted to calling escorts on average once a month. His girlfriend knew none of this at the time. The last four years of their relationship Brian disclosed he and his girlfriend had sex four times (once a year on average). The relationship ended because his girlfriend cheated on him and he found out. This crushed him!

Since then Brian has been in a stream of non-intimate relationships lasting about three months. He still calls escorts and visits strip clubs. He states he has a strong sexual desire and wants to continue to have sex. He also states he does not trust women and has no value for women. Brian also discloses that his relationship with his mother was very distant and that as a child he remembers being scolded by her often and trying to win her affection in multiple ways. Brain left therapy when he started to really discuss his relationship with his mother. He was not ready to confront his issues.

One of the things Brian disclosed in a couple therapy sessions had to do with his arousal toward strippers, call girls and escorts. There was no doubt that these women turned him on! Curiously, he claimed to get aroused more leading up to planning the encounters with them rather than the actual sex! In fact, Brian discussed how much sexual discomfort he would be in, driving to where he would meet his "date". Furthermore he also stated that sometimes he would be so aroused and "hard" going to meet the woman, but upon arriving, he would be flaccid. This happened a couple of times. Brian said he started taking sexual stimulants prior to meeting these women to "not look like a loser" ever again!

Eventually Brian had to go back to therapy, since he was missing so much work over the last few months due to porn viewing, doing drugs and using the services of pay-for-play girls in the middle of the night. It was actually a couple of the girls Brian was paying for sex, that introduced him to drugs.

Upon listening to Brian's story and the series of his events leading to him returning to therapy, the therapist believed Brian had an addictive personality.

Brian's therapist asked him point blank if he believed he was a sex addict. After a few days of deliberating, Brian returned to the next session and claimed by all accounts he was, given the large amount of porn he also reported watching. Brian's days had basically revolved around sex -- viewing porn, thinking about sex all of the time, checking out women conspicuously as well as taking risky chances including letting things interfere with his career.

Brian also asserted that he was purging himself of the bad inside with the pay-for-play girls, in that when a woman who was relationship material came into his life, he would be able to commit and give her 100% of himself!

Brian clearly demonstrates the Madonna complex in his inability to commit to a lasting intimate relationship with any of the females he had been intimate with. In addition, Brian is clearly compulsive with sex and has been for a while now. Interestingly, Brian divulged something that addicts often times experience, especially gamblers. It wasn't the experience of having sex which most turned Brian on, rather the anticipation of having sex. Similarly, problematic gamblers often report that it isn't the gambling (game) itself that arouse them, but rather the planning and anticipation leading up to attending the casino or playing their game!

The chase or pursuit of the substance, sex or gambling is often times more paramount to the addict than the substance itself. Many sex addicts report finding or playing a woman to have sex with, is more fulfilling than the orgasm they experience!

We interviewed a few people on the concept of sex addiction/sexual compulsivity and here is what they had to say:

Corrin:

"Yes I believe people can become addicted to sex. There are people out there that can become addicted to anything -- exercise, food, drugs, you name it! Like any other addictions, sex addiction needs treatment too! I don't know what the actual type of treatment is for sex addicts. Is there AA for sex addiction?"

Jack:

"Yes, I am addicted to sex -- I love it! No, seriously I do like sex but I don't think I'm addicted to it. I think people can become addicted to it, just like anything else. I don't know if I believe in the Madonna complex though, because I really don't understand it. How could you not want to have sex with your wife -- you married her! I guess it would be cool to have sex with your wife and anyone else you wanted to, but then I wouldn't want her to do the same thing. So you are either single or in a relationship – people need to choose!"

Justin:

"I believe that people can become compulsive with sex and literally destroy their lives. My cousin did. He was married and used the services of prostitutes often. His wife caught him and took everything including the kids. He now has no house, no money and his ex wife does not want him to have contact with the kids. I don't know if he even cares because I know he is still picking up prostitutes. Now that we are talking about the Madonna complex -- I think he might have this issue!"

At the beginning of this chapter we posed the notion of whether or not sex can become an addiction. There is no doubt that it can. For the nay sayers who assert the only time it seems to be used as an "addiction" is when married people get caught... Especially famous celebrities. Not the case!

There are many individuals in support groups and therapy sessions for sex addictions. Many of them entered their treatment 100% single. They possessed addictive personalities and sex became their vice!

Married men who possess the Madonna complex deal with a two-headed monster. First, they cheat on their mates because they seek out another woman to fulfill their sexual desires and fantasies. Second, some of these men get addicted to the sex they have with their "whores" and need more!

A married man can possess the Madonna complex and not be addicted to sex. He uses the sexual services of mistresses or prostitutes in moderation and can go without for periods of time, just as his own wife is forced to. On the other hand, a married man possessing the Madonna complex, who is addicted to sex, has some extreme issues he needs to resolve. He is already cheating which is very wrong. Addicts in this case compulsively cheat which makes the likelihood of them getting caught more likely. This will most likely end up with their marriage/family getting destroyed as well as potential serious financial liabilities. Also, if he is engaging in sex with multiple partners liberally, he may contract a sexually transmitted disease and even pass it on to his wife.

Sex addictions are real. Sex addictions can pose serious problems not only for the individual possessing the addiction, but those tied to the sex addict as well. They say that with any addiction, the hardest part is for the individual to acknowledge that they have an addiction. That is roughly 50% of the battle! The 50% is getting the treatment, which many claim is the easier side of the coin because one's mind is geared towards getting fixed.

The problem with a sex addiction is so many continue to do it because it feels good, they are not getting drunk or drugged up, and in their mind, no one is getting hurt. Some believe it is a basic necessity just as eating is. That is true, but a married person who eats incessantly may become portly, but he has stayed faithful to his spouse. On the other hand one who has a sex addiction and steps out of their marriage has violated a bond of both trust and respect.

As we close out this chapter, it is important to note that some married men who cheat a lot on their wives and who also admit they are sex addicts may not seek professional help because of disclosure issues. Obviously, they don't want their wives finding out, but they also worry who they might run into at the support groups. Most try to quit on their own and really want to quit to avoid the embarrassment and repercussions, but the truth is, if it really were that easy, they would have quit a long time ago. They wouldn't have waited until it got so far out of hand!

CHAPTER SUMMARY -- KEY POINTS

1) A sex addiction is defined as a psychological condition where the individual (male or female) has an inability to manage their sexual behaviour.

2) An addiction exists when an individual has tried repeatedly on their own to quit but can't!

3) Anything that numbs the pain (emotional or physical) can become compulsive and used as a way of distracting themselves from their problems. Sex addicts use sex.

4) A married man can possess the Madonna complex and not be addicted to sex. Men who possess the Madonna complex and are sex addicts are more likely to get caught cheating eventually .

CHAPTER TEN

TREATMENT

ACCEPTANCE

& FORGIVENESS

Forgiving is love's toughest work, and love's biggest risk. If you twist it into something it was never meant to be, it can make you a doormat or an insufferable manipulator. Forgiving seems almost unnatural. Our sense of fairness tells us people should pay for the wrong they do. But forgiving is love's power to break nature's rule.

Lewis B. Smedes

The Madonna complex is something that is real. It is not made up to protect one's reputation or psyche after getting caught cheating on one's spouse. There are however some who will feign the qualities of the Madonna complex in order to try and avoid the consequences of their actions, but they are few! Who wants to admit they cheat or engage in perverse sexual acts because they have a sex addiction or the Madonna complex? Not too many men would be proud enough to admit this. The main question then becomes this: Is the Madonna complex like any other mental health illness or addiction? Whether it is a mental health illness or not, how do you treat it? And what about the spouse who gets cheated on, namely one's wife? Is she just suppose to accept it, forgive it and forget it?

Western society today has become all about sex. No matter where you look, there seems to be something "sexy" hanging in the foreground or lurking in the background. Bottom line: Sex sells! With that said, people will always be tempted when it comes to having sex or at least fantasizing about it. Unfortunately, some married men and some committed in relationships are likely to snap at the bait and bite in. Before they know it, it's too late! They have stepped out on their spouse and did the unthinkable for both.

With regards to the Madonna complex, due to the problems that happen both intra-personally and inter-personally, there needs to be some sort of treatment if a man wants to have a healthy and sexually exclusive monogamous relationship with his partner. If he ever wants to have a well-balanced relationship based on trust, loyalty and intimacy with his partner, he first has to establish harmony within himself.

The question of whether or not the Madonna complex can be treated is one that many disagree on. The fact that this complex is so deeply-rooted in childhood relationships to mothers, is one of the caveats to treatment. Much of the research related to the Madonna complex focuses on the deep unconscious mind, the place where the seeds of this complex reside and have taken root. Getting to the root cause, accepting what has happened in the past and dealing with it, makes treatment for this complex a daunting task!

We have focussed much of our work on the psychoanalytic prospective of the Madonna complex. Coming to grips with what happened in childhood is accomplished through a variety of psychoanalytical methods. This approach usually relies on years of therapy and involves resolving unfinished business which was a by-product of being/feeling rejected by one's mother. Psychoanalysts may choose regression methods such as hypnosis and/free associations to tap into the unconscious. Let's face it, most people don't want to spend years trying to undo and replace the bad years in their lives, as that is not truly living!

There are a few other ideas about the distinctness of this complex. One such theory resides more on a Primal theory of sorts. Primal theory is the theory that in general looks at repressed pain that individuals hold onto. That repressed pain divides the person into two distinct parts of the self. The end result is these two sides end up in a battle with one another for control over the mind. This battle is what causes torment in the human being.

The Madonna complex from this perspective is a bit different from the psychodynamic perspective where the male child has repressed love feelings for his mother left over from unresolved issues in the Oedipus complex. The primal explanation to this complex is somewhat of the opposite. The male child has repressed feelings for his mother because his mother never met his needs as a child. So essentially the adult male unconsciously connects his wife to that of his mother who never met his needs for love and affection. He then plays out his early infancy needs, with his wife, which are not sexual by any means.

What starts to happen from these unmet needs is that the husband begins to have unrealistic expectations from his wife as he essentially is unconsciously searching for his mother within his wife. The next thing to develop within his mind are intimacy issues. These intimacy issues could be seen as a defence mechanism -- to not re-experience the pain he felt in childhood. The pain is often that of neglect. It is primarily because of this that the husband stops not only sexual intimacy, but even emotional intimacy with his wife. He tries to create as much emotional distance from her as possible as she serves as a trigger to his perceived past rejections and failures involving his mother.

The primary mode of treatment for the Madonna complex is psychotherapy. Unfortunately this complex is not something that can be masked with a pill. Like many other mental health issues we come into contact with "a pill" that is going to "fix" the issue. Often times men with the Madonna complex do turn to pills and booze as ways for hiding the shame, guilt and hurt they are feeling within. Furthermore, it is even less common for the married men to engage in even more affairs as a form of self-destructive behaviour -- some actually wish to get caught to spare their wives further hurt!

THE THERAPEUTIC PROCESS

When most couples attend the first counselling session, wives usually complain about the lack of sex they have in their marriage/relationship. The couple is usually in discord and close to divorce/separation because of the lack of intimacy in the relationship. Wives are usually in great doubt about themselves which can often times be a separate therapeutic issue that will need to be dealt with aside. This self doubt stems from the lack of intimacy in the relationship where the woman begin (and ends) feeling unworthy of her husband's/partner's affection. She then begins to doubt her physical worth, emotional worth, and mental worth. This doubt eventually turns into anger and resentment with the end result of shutting down all aspects of herself. We will discuss her process as we go on.

Often times the couple will be split up in therapy where the husband will come separately and the wife may be advised to seek individual counselling or the therapist may choose to see her separately as well. There is also work the couple will do outside of the counselling sessions. Both parties will be asked to complete genograms to gain better insights into their pasts. Genograms are hereditary pattern flow charts which show psychological factors that punctuate relationships at certain periods in a person's life. Genograms are excellent tools for identifying repetitive patterns of behavior in not only one's own relationships and self, but from parents and grandparents as well. Therapists will work through the genograms with the couple creating a situation whereby everyone feels like they are learning about each other for the first time. This also encourages communication between spouses while at the same time creating the antecedent for emotional intimacy.

The goal of therapy is for both husbands and wives to understand what the Madonna complex is, how it started and how to change existing destructive relationship patterns to increase communication and emotional intimacy.

It is imperative to have a full understanding of the Madonna complex before the couple begins building or rebuilding their intimacy.

Often times the process is much more difficult because of potential for secondary issues stemming from the Madonna complex. One such is sex addiction/ sexual compulsivity. This is essentially a way for the husband to act out, which is a way for him to avoid the anxiety around not only his repressed feelings about his mother, but also the confrontations with his wife.

The wife/partner of the man with the Madonna complex suffers in a number of ways. Primarily she is neglected in the areas of intimacy both physical and emotional. The common advice to women is to leave the relationship ASAP! Sometimes knee-jerk reactions such as ending a relationship immediately creates more unfinished business and greater resentment in both husbands and wives. Sometimes it is better to hold on and try to at least work through the issues with professional guidance. Of course the female partner has to have a full understanding of the Madonna complex in order to begin to understand where and how her husband/partner got to the point he is. She will usually turn her head to the infidelity of her husband as a way to cope with it. This leads her to feeling helpless, hopeless and with no direction in her life. All of this has to be repaired!

With that being said, the majority of the work falls on the male. It is he who has to learn how the complex developed, accept that he has the complex and be willing to do the work to resolve the deep rooted issues he holds. If he chooses not to resolve the issues then his relationship will end. The Madonna complex is not something where a man can force himself to have sex with his partner and think it will just go away. It does not! When a man tries to create a "normal" relationship to save his marriage or relationship in order to appease his wife, he often times winds up with erectile dysfunction issues (secondary sexual dysfunctions).

Also it should be pointed out that the husband shouldn't be getting help to "try and save the marriage". Instead, he should be getting therapy because he feels he is thinking and behaving irrationally which is causing stress in the marriage. He needs to get help to help himself -- he can't change for his wife!

The work usually involves psychotherapy (talk therapy). All significant relationships need to be discussed in great detail from childhood. Patterns of anger, hostility, neglect (emotional and physical), dependence and emptiness, all need to be examined in the male's life. In addition, education of what a healthy emotional relationship is, and what a healthy physical relationship is, needs to be analyzed. Boundaries for the self and boundaries with others need to be explored. If there are any other issues that arise in the therapy sessions, then they need to be worked through as well. These can be anything from secondary sexual dysfunctions to personality disorders, to mood disorders and so on.

Often the partner may need to do her own individual work (therapy) to rebuild her self-esteem, self-awareness, and self-worth. In addition she will need to repair how she feels about herself as a sexual being after all the rejection she has faced in her relationship. Often times, the female partner may feel like giving up, as visible change in her partner is usually very slow. Any intimate relationships she has outside of her marriage/relationship that she used as a way to deal with the emotional and physical neglect from her husband/partner also need to be cut off immediately!

We interviewed a few women on the topic and here's what they had to say:

Maggie:

"If my boyfriend or husband stopped having sex with me I would probably leave him. I really don't want to put up with that crap nor do I want to mother some guy whether I love him or not!"

Jennifer:

"Wait, there is really such a thing? That is crazy! How and why would any woman put up with that? That's really damaging. If my husband had the Madonna complex I would probably divorce him. I don't think I could get over his affairs and the way he looks at women. If I chose a guy like that, I think I would need therapy for making such a bad decision!"

Jordan:

I had no idea there was a disorder like this. I am going to go home and Google it! My opinion is a man who has this complex will never be satisfied with a woman, which will ultimately result in him never being satisfied with life! If he is unable to bond on all levels in terms of intimacy with his woman, then he may feel less adequate as a human being due to the pressures of society to have a loving and healthy relationship which constitutes an active and satisfying sex life in addition to a true love connection."

Accepting and forgiving is a large part of recovery for both partners in this situation. A man has to forgive and heal from his childhood situations with his mother and learn to accept her for who she is/was. It is through this healing process that he can begin to move on and learn about his unhealthy sexual and relational behaviour with women. The man has to learn through the process of forgiving his mother how to forgive *ALL* women. He has to learn to trust women and accept women for who they are as women.

If the female partner makes the decision to stay with her mate, then she has to accept him for everything he is and has been, and learn to forgive his past behaviours. The mindset is *ACCEPTING, FORGIVING,* and *MOVING FORWARD.* This can be very difficult for the female to do because of the amount of pain she endured throughout the relationship. However, only when she truly understands the Madonna complex is when she can start to heal as well!

*There are a variety and variations of treatments to treat aspects of the Madonna complex, sex addictions and couples counselling. We did not get into them as we would have had to write at least 10 books which explore these methods within their own rights.

Since the Madonna complex is not well-understood, often times individuals may have to see a host of treatments concurrently to get help. The best place to start is the Internet. Ironically, those with the Madonna complex who use the Internet to engage in their porn addictions have only ever been just a few keys away from typing in words in a Google search which could greatly help them. It is never too late! Currently, there are excellent forums and chatrooms on-line for sex addicts and those who possess aspects of the Madonna complex. Most communities now have support groups as well for sex addictions. If you feel you are destroying your marriage it isn't too late to get help before things get worse!

CHAPTER SUMMARY - KEY POINTS

1) A man with the Madonna complex, due to the problems that happen both intra-personally and inter-personally, needs treatment if he wants to have a healthy and sexually exclusive monogamous relationship with his partner.

2) Primal theory is the theory that in general looks at repressed pain that individuals hold onto. That repressed pain divides the person into two distinct parts of the self and these two sides ends up in a battle with one another for control of the mind.

3) Genograms are excellent tools for identifying repetitive patterns of behavior in not only one's own relationships and self, but from parents and grandparents as well.

4) The goal of therapy is for both husbands and wives to understand what the Madonna complex is, how it started and how to change existing destructive relationship patterns to increase communication and emotional intimacy.

CHAPTER ELEVEN

INTERNET DATING:

THE NEW

MADONNA

COMPLEX

I can have all the sex I want at the press of a button. It's always safe, I never have to spend a dime on dinner or drinks, or any of that intimacy crap. As long as my Internet service provider gets my monthly cheque, everyone is always satisfied--keeps me cumming back for more!

Author unknown

After the completion of this book, it is amazing how serendipitous things have a way of happening. In this case, world's collided--Madonna Complex and Internet dating. It was interesting to hear people relay their stories after the fact which included their own Madonna Complex experiences. More interestingly, another wrinkle was occurring which involved people finding or searching for relationships through Internet dating only to find the people they were meeting had aspects of the Madonna Complex, or they themselves possessed these similar aspects.

Internet Dating Junkies

After reading our book on the Madonna Complex you should have a solid idea of the ins and outs of the issues that some men deal with regarding their sexuality. Keep in mind that these men place women into two distinct categories; 1) women who they want as their girlfriend or wife and, 2) women they want to have causal and perhaps kinky or perverse sex with. In order for a man to want the female as his girlfriend or wife she has to possess "good" moral character as well as behaviours that resemble those that his mother displays. Since we already knew this, we were curious to see how it effects the way people date today and most commonly find mates. Since it is estimated that 60-70% of people today try Internet dating, we questioned what role the Internet plays in the Madonna Complex?

Before we begin our analysis we will discuss Internet dating first and some of the common features of the online dating world. There were plenty of questions that came up for us with regard to the high rate of

Internet dating users, the easy access to dating sites (both paid and free), and the enormous rate of compulsive sexual behaviour that we found (People mentioned this to us from the online dating sites they used.).

Compulsive sexual behaviour (CSB) also known as "sex addiction" refers to a propensity one has towards extreme and often times prolonged sexual behaviours which can be damaging to one self, relationships and others involved in the addict's life. Throughout much of the research presented on compulsive sexual behaviour, one thing is crystal clear -- the addict jeopardizes the ability to obtain and maintain what would be considered normal social and emotional bonds with other people! Perhaps the word normal is loosely used these days and for that matter it doesn't mean much of anything. For the purpose of argument, "normal" in this case equates with behaviour that would be considered beneficial, as well as healthy (mentally, emotionally, physically and spiritually) for the individual. Humans are social by nature and need social as well as emotional contact.

While it is true that there is much controversy surrounding the concept of compulsive sexual behaviour leaving many people, both professional and lay with differing opinions, there is no doubt that it does truly exist! One such criticism with regard to compulsive sexual behaviour is the concern in handing out diagnoses for CSB-- It projects unclear social stigmas onto people rooted in the Victorian era for what is right and what is wrong. This is where the enigma in regard to what truly is a sex addiction never really gets resolved. Ah, the magic and chemistry of sex!

Get this! The reality is more than 1/4 million American people watch 11 hours plus of pornography daily, with the number one Internet search being "sex", and roughly more than 20 million people visit online dating sites a month. Those are some serious numbers folks! What are these people looking for, or truly hoping to find? Are they sex addicts looking to feed their lustful addictions, or are they the curious in line to be the next conglomerate of sex addicts after repeated exposure? Those who visit dating sites are not necessarily addicted to sex or pornography, however we raise the question... Are they addictive personality types, or can become addicted to Internet dating sites? Good question!

We wondered how and why Internet dating can lead to compulsive behaviours. We examined some of studies done on Facebook and other social networking sites. Indeed, we found that people do in fact become compulsive with social networking and perhaps "surfing" the Internet in general. Here are some of the statistics about Facebook taken from Facebook's statistics page:

* More than 750 million active users

* Average user has 130 friends

* People spend over 700 billion minutes per month on Facebook.

*There are more than 250 million active users accessing Facebook through their mobile devices

It is no secret that those people who are active on Facebook and other sites are searching the site regularly, often times multiple visits a day, and mobile users are generally twice as active on Facebook. It is believed that active Facebook users tend to be more compulsive with the site. In addition we have heard many of our interviewees state how compelled they become using Facebook, feeling like they are missing out on something if they are not searching or posting on the site. Interestingly, some even complain of withdrawal symptoms when they go prolonged periods of time without using Facebook and other social networking sites! And now the dating sites--

Most people start out with good intentions when it comes to Internet dating. There may be no love connections where they live or perhaps "dry" with respect to the dating scene. So they go on one of the many dating sites available on-line to search for a connection, friendship and hopefully love. We have to "side bar" here because we want to bring to your attention the difference between the sex sites that are often wrapped up in "dating site wrapping paper" and actual dating sites. Yes there is a big difference, or is there? Usually and ultimately people not only want companionship but they also want to have a physical sexual relationship. The goal of any dating site is just that. Yes sex is involved! Yet there are some sites that are little more forthcoming with how they approach sex in the sense that companionship usually takes a back seat. Even with the more reputable dating sites there are plenty of people doing what we like to call "sex searching."

Peter's book on dating, *FAST FOOD DATING YOUR 2 CENTS: OVER 1000 SERVED*, explores the categories of Internet daters. Peter actually interviewed and/or worked with major dating sites and services to collect information. Here is an excerpt from the book with best describes the categories:

1) The Naughties

I sought out sex and pornography forums and chats to purposely meet people because that was what I was there to do.

2) The Easily Swayed

My prolonged participation on the Internet desensitized me because of who I was chatting with or curiosity led me to forums I did not initially seek out. This eventually led me to chat more with "naughty people" seeking sex.

3) The Curious

After a while I got tired of not meeting who I was looking for so I decided to check out how the naughty half lives. Who knows, Mr. (Ms.) Right might not be there so what's wrong with finding Mr. (Ms.) Right Now?

4) The Steadfast

As long as I have been using the Internet for dating, I have never sought out a sexual relationship nor do I consider it, or even look in the domains where I can find these people.

We were not really shocked or surprised how the responses came out. Interestingly, it seemed everyone had at some point chatted with someone looking for sex on the Internet. This is not to say they themselves were there looking. The Naughties were definitely there looking for sex. Many of those we interviewed were already in a committed relationship but sought sex outside their relationship. Most informed us it was extremely easy to meet people for sex on the Internet and be successful in what they were looking for.

The Easily Swayed and the Curious were more likely to have chatted with or even sought out people on-line looking for sex. Many sighted boredom, frustration and just plain curiosity/fantasy as their reasoning for seeking sex partners and/or cyber sex. Funny, some actually believed they could find a "diamond in the rough" and convert "him" back to a respectable man. Many women asserted that if you met a man in the first place on-line who was looking for sex, even if you were to develop a serious relationship with them, they would always be looking for more on-line. Men felt the same way about women surfing the Net for sex. More than half of the people we interviewed in these two categories were still chatting with people looking for sex or they themselves had converted over on occasion or permanently into the sex/one night stand category, or already had an encounter of this type from their participation in Internet dating.

The Steadfast group reflected what their name meant for the most part. Some did visit websites or forums to read profiles of those looking for sex, but almost all who did claimed it was out of a morbid sense of curiosity. They believed most if not all people on the Internet looking for sexual relationships were all players and liars. They were content to remain single rather than compromising their ideals and being hurt, disappointed or heart-broken.

(From Fast Food Dating Your 2 Cents 2007)

So when we are looking at compulsive behaviour and dating sites, or for that matter any online social networking site (which in essence can become a dating playground) we examined some of the very interesting habits of people who engage them. These would include:

A modest to severe level of exhibitionism- Generally defined as exposing one's genitals or any sexual organ including breasts and buttocks to unsuspecting people. This interest is linked under the category of compulsive sexual behaviour (sex addiction). You can visit a countless number of dating sites and social networking sites and find a whole host of pictures from nude to suggestive sexual pictures.

A modest to severe level of voyeurism- Voyeurism is defined as the sexual interest or practice of spying on people engaged in intimate behaviours such as undressing or some sort of sexual activity. When a person is on a dating or social networking site they are essentially acting in a voyeuristic fashion. On these sites we want to know what people are doing, what they are wearing, what their interests are, where they were yesterday, etc. It is also interesting to note that voyeurism falls under the category of compulsive sexual behaviour (sex addiction).

Pressure for social etiquette- Another habit and for that matter a pattern of "Internet Junkies" is a real sense of etiquette when it comes to posting and responding. If someone posts on your wall most people feel the pressure to respond back just like verbal communication. This is also at the core of the compulsion. In the Internet dating and social networking world this is called reciprocity.

The belief that everyone on the site is your friend or a potential date- Many people go into the Internet world believing that they can and do have a connection with everyone and anyone online. This is also where the dishonesty can stem from. By now we all know that many people deceive with their photos and lie about their age as well as what they are interested in. There is a false sense of reality for many. There is a subtle sense of compulsion when it comes to finding the one that is real.

The posting of pictures and personal information as well as the searching of these personal pictures and information is exactly what some become obsessed with. There is a sophisticated game of ping pong going on between some peoples' voyeuristic and exhibitionist tendencies. That accompanies the pressure to engage/respond as well as the belief that there are countless connections. At some point the obsessed begin doing what they have to in order to get the connection they so desperately want, even if it means lying.

Where does the Madonna Complex come into play in Internet dating? And does it affect men only or women as well? What exactly is the Madonna Complex for Internet dating? And does it all have to do with sex or does it foster relationships and/or friendships as well?

MADONNA COMPLEX AND INTERNET DATING

When it comes to the Madonna Complex and Internet dating, 5 things happen.

1) A need in the real world (non-cyber world) isn't being met and Internet is an option, best option or only option. People believe this is the best way to meet someone for

whatever they hope to achieve; friendships, dating, relationships or sex.

2) The Internet dating platform serves as the magic lantern or the genie who will grant wishes--Love or lust! Since there is the great ability to be anonymous and it is highly convenient, the opportunities to fulfill fantasies are endless. Remember, so much of cyber play (on-line dating and for sure sex) is based on fantasy and role-playing. People get to "test-drive" what types of fantasies they want with others, mostly people they do not know or will ever meet in person.

3) Internet daters get to "practice" on-line who and what they want to be. Funny, but it is not uncommon for people to try out different identities and personas to see what not only works best in attracting others, but also to see what they perceive as being most comfortable. Some people become like "shape-shifters", the creatures most commonly found in vampire novels, but they take on different personhoods on-line to see which will bring them the greatest success in meeting others, or having their fantasies fulfilled.

4) Over time, too many Internet daters grow tired, bored, frustrated or desensitized to the sites. The best intentions of meeting someone go to pot! They may have met someone or several dates early on in person, but with repeated sessions on-line coupled with "fantasy seeking" whether it be their ideal mate for a relationship or sex, the lustre starts to wear off and they are continually looking for something better. Here is where the Madonna Complex begins--fantasy overrides intention!

What happens is many people become habituated or addicted to the site over time looking for their ideal mate. Since it is like a supermarket or ocean of possibilities for meeting, there is always that, "What if there is someone better and just around the corner?". This becomes the new intention. "I will keep looking for my ideal partner no matter how long it takes." The mindset changes to "keep looking", or "they must be out there" and "I need to keep looking." Unfortunately, the longer one stays on a dating site, especially over a long period of time and if they engage the site daily for let's say 21-28 days consecutively, they become hooked! It no longer becomes a matter of meeting "Mr. Right", it is more like "looking for Mr. Right" and making comparisons. In doing so, comparisons cause confusion and chaos. Why? No one is perfect! No one will measure up to the fantasy at this point. So, what Internet daters start to do is look for only the "good", which are the best parts of people they engage on the sites and hope to find those "best parts" all rolled into one. This is when ego comes in--

Prolonged Internet daters believe the perfect mate is out there for them. Come hell or high water, they will meet this person. As frustration seeps in from repeated failures (no one measures up to their ideal mate), the fantasy of "Mr. Right" or "Mrs. Right" becomes more satisfying. At this point they become more cynical of dating and meeting the ideal person and the dating site takes on a whole new purpose. In reality, the Internet dating site becomes like a cyber-bar or cyber nightclub, hosting barflies which only adds to one's frustration in finding the right person. Ironically, the Internet dating junkie who is looking for their "ideal mate" eventually over time becomes one of these flies!

5) Eventually an addiction to Internet dating occurs due to compromise and frustration. With the best of intentions laid at the outset--finding the right person to have a relationship with, months and years of disappointment, frustration and/or sexual meetings lead to an addiction to Internet dating sites. What happens,

the dating sites become a form of recreation or entertainment for some, but for addictive personalities a lifestyle! The Internet site is their own personal brand of heroin or whiskey. It gives them what they believe they need or what is missing in their life. Some people literally go into withdrawal if they miss a day not being able to chat on-line! The wheels literally fall off and much like a kid who is hooked on video games, they become hooked on Internet dating sites. The irony of this is overtime they could care less about going out and actually meeting. Instead they would rather talk and fantasize on line with whom they could have met in person. This spares them greater disappointment and they feel they save themselves from having to invest the effort of meeting in person.

From our interviews, we should also point out that by this point, many people are willing to compromise themselves as well as their ideals for who they hoped to meet. They find themselves having sexual affairs (out of character for them), or dating/relating to people they would never have thought of being around in their wildest dreams. They are miserable being around these people but their ego convinces them that, "Something is better than nothing!" and that they are, "Not a failure, rather lovable." Basically, those who go about getting into relationships this way wind up in situations for all of the wrong reasons, much like the Madonna Complex marriages.

AFFECTS ON MEN AND WOMEN

When it comes to men and women, the Madonna Complex does not discriminate in terms of Internet dating. It is estimated that both men and women use Internet dating sites in terms of equal percentages, but men are more likely to use the sites geared toward sex or pornography, and with women using traditional Internet dating venues. It should be pointed out that when we were interviewing people for this book, as well as when Peter was interviewing people for *Fast Food Dating Your 2 Cents* more women commented that they were using the Internet dating sites for sexual encounters as well. It seems today women are more liberal in their searches/quests for on-line sex.

When men use Internet dating for sex, many get hooked on it! In fact, the fulfillment of fantasies from having cyber-sex is often times more appealing than actually meeting women. The fantasy and their ability to control the situation on-line holds better merit than actually meeting or even having sex in real life. When this happens early on for young men and teens, this has the potential to lead to the Madonna Complex in their marriage or relationships. They will still feel the need to be on-line surfing the web and fantasizing.

Women on the other hand are more likely to create idealized fantasies of meeting Mr. Right. They want the perfect man for them who won't disappoint them--abuse, cheat, hurt or let them down. In a lot of cases, women who hold these fantasies and expectations have recently come out of abusive relationships or have experienced years of abuse and because of their dysfunctional mindsets many still hold, they continually attract the same kind of men--abusers, cheats, liars, etc. This is the Law of Attraction/Law of Intention at work in their lives. Is it any wonder they choose to just "chat/date" on-line without ever meeting? At some point they lose faith in the dating process and are content to live out their fantasies on-line.

MADONNA COMPLEX FOR INTERNET DATING

When the Madonna Complex occurs for Internet daters is when reality loses its foothold and the addiction/obsession to the fantasy becomes overwhelming. The Internet dater crosses a threshold believing a "perfect partner" exists and can only stop Internet dating all-together when they meet this person. However meeting this "perfect partner" becomes entirely cumbersome over time. At some point searching becomes addictive. Some might call it an obsession to find the right person, but needing to be on-line continuously becomes the addictive aspect. The underlying, embedded issue to the fantasy however is addiction. The individual becomes addicted to Internet dating!

They may meet the person of their dreams and really be in love with the person they have met, but they can't seem to break away from the Internet dating sites. They begin to surmise this must mean they do not love or like the person they are with, at least not enough, or else they wouldn't be on the site. Love and like has nothing to do with their mate and why they continually use the site. What has happened is they became addicted to the site with repeated use. They could love many people over time (for sex addicts it would be lust) but not be able to break free from needing to be on Internet dating sites.

The problem occurs when the person is unable to accept they have an addiction/compulsion--to Internet dating. As long as their ego gets in the way (denying they are hooked/addicted to the Internet) the cycle will continually repeat. We found people from our interviews who have been Internet dating for more than a decade now!

IT'S NOT ALL ABOUT SEX

Internet dating and the Madonna Complex is not all about sex. In the case of it being the Internet, it does not have to be about cyber-sex! It is more about fantasy leading to compulsion. Remember, the longer you engage in something the more likely you are going to develop a habit or addiction to it. It takes no more than 4 weeks roughly to become hooked on something. If you start Internet dating and continue to do it for a month and start to feel "the need to be on it", that is a good sign you are becoming habituated to it. You do not need to be having sex or being sexually aroused to be hooked or addicted to it.

There is so much more we could share with you in this chapter on Internet dating addiction tied to the Madonna Complex, but the chapter would fast become an entire book on its own merit! With that, we will close out this chapter with the following case study/interviews we conducted.

The common case is that of Robert:

Robert was a forty-two year old male who was newly single. Because of Robert's recent divorce his friends talked him into trying out some online dating services since he was concerned about going to bars and meeting people for what he thought of to be the only social scene out there for dating.

Robert joined three online dating sites, two of them with monthly fees and the other one was free. Robert would search occasionally and get "hits." Hits being when someone checks out your profile and sends you a message of interest. After his divorce Robert felt like he didn't know how to talk to females and felt a bit apprehensive about dating. The online dating seemed to fit him better in the sense that he felt he could get to know someone in the privacy of his own home without the social anxiety he was concerned about.

Robert explained that once he got his first hit he was hooked. He started spending more time on all three dating sites and found himself communicating with twelve women at one time. He would go out occasionally and meet women from the dating site but found he liked (and got a rush from) talking to women online.

Robert also found himself on the dating sites while at work which was affecting his productivity. Robert explained that he felt like he had to see what was going on constantly with the women he was connected to. He was focused on looking at their profiles consistently, browsing their new pictures and even focusing in on one of their pictures and masturbating to it. He even found himself downloading one of the pictures and saving it as a screen saver on his computer. Robert admitted to his compulsion.

One of the most interesting things that can stem from Internet dating is a total loss of, and avoidance for real face to face relationships. Often times compulsive Internet daters lose the capacity to have real emotional and physical intimacy with a real person. There is a level of anonymity that the Internet provides which means they will generally hide themselves from the reality of true intimacy. It is essentially escapism which allows people to retreat into an imaginary world.

Another issue is that people will also substitute the online world for real world relationships. Friends and love interests become masked behind a computer screen (also mobile devices these days). Deep connection is often times lost in the shuffle. The ability to look into someone's eyes and read their body language never becomes a part of the development of the relationship.

Though many people believe they have a deep connection with the people they meet it is a façade. Spending all of one's time on the Internet becomes self destructive, perhaps even dangerous for some! Neglecting work, everyday activities, family, and even personal hygiene is at the core of the danger.

Shauna reported the following:

Internet dating was a great way for me to meet guys because of my busy schedule and because I am not into the bar scene. I was doing it for a couple of years and have had both my good encounters with it and bad encounters. In the beginning, I think I was like most people who see a movie like "You've Got Mail" and you think your soul mate is out there somewhere. You start thinking about love and romance very much like a career. If you apply a strong work ethic to your career, you'll be successful. Maybe I believed the same about Internet dating in that if I worked hard and was persistent, then the same rules would apply for love. If I tilled the land, I would harvest a fine crop. Unfortunately, I would have to say I have been more disappointed and let down than pleasantly surprised. I am not knocking everyone I have met because I am sure they were great guys, but my expectations were a little higher. I am sure these guys could be saying the same about me.

What really bothered me the most is spending all this time on the Internet and phone, and sometimes it was months, anticipating the actual meeting. You finally meet the person, who you might even think you are in love with. The worst has to be seeing the person and having zero physical attraction and chemistry. You can feel the pit of your stomach drop out. Or when you engage in a conversation and then see them going south quickly, remotely resembling anything like the Internet or phone chats you previously had with them. I am sure nerves have a lot to do with it when you finally meet, but there is a whole different kind of chemistry involved. You either have it or you bomb out and it sucks!

CHAPTER SUMMARY - KEY POINTS

1) Internet dating is one of the most popular method people are using to meet others of friendship, dating, romance and sex. In many cases, they start out with the best of intentions but become quickly jaded by their experience or compromise their intentions.

2) The Madonna Complex is very applicable to Internet dating. The more time people invest on a daily basis the more likely they are to become addicted to Internet or develop a compulsion to it. Over a period of time and energy, one's ego becomes clouded and Internet dating users find themselves hooked on the fantasy of meeting someone rather than actually meeting them.

3) The Madonna Complex affects both men and women when it comes to Internet dating. Men are more likely to engage in Internet dating sites for sexual fantasies, while women are more likely to use the dating sites for romantic/love fantasies. Even though over time many complain they hate Internet dating and vow never to do it again, they find themselves back on-line and can't stop!

AFTER THOUGHTS

or...

AFTER SHOCKS?

Today is the first day of the rest of your life.

Anonymous

The Madonna complex is something that is...Very complex! After reading this book we're sure there are women out there who still don't believe in it. We're sure there are also men who concur. From our interviews and research, many asserted the Madonna complex is nothing more than a self-serving, pop psychology term-of-the-day, used by men who get caught putting their penises where they shouldn't. Perhaps!

After researching material for this book, conducting interviews and asking other professionals what they thought, we came to several conclusions:

1) From the beginning of time up until the current time period we are existing in, women are still in "damned if they do" and "damned if they don't" positions. If women act/dress provocatively or sexy, they are seen as potential "whores". When they let their hair down and become sexual with more than one man, then they usually get "whore" status! Conversely, if they remain prim and proper (avoid looking or acting the sexual part), most men, even women find them boring!

2) Women are expected to play two roles; "woman" and "caregiver". When a man feels sexual, he wants a "sexy" woman. When a man wants to play family man, he expects a woman to be "mother" and "caregiver" to both him and his kids. Even though androgyny is more prevalent in today's world, men are not forced to be "father" figures as much as women are expected to be mothers.

3) Men have double standards for infidelity. When a married man has a sexual affair, it is just that... Sex. When a married woman has sex, it must mean something more... Emotional intimacy. If it is "just sex" for men, then he is only having a sexual encounter and fulfilling a need his wife isn't meeting, or he is sparing her of the gory act! Conversely, if a wife steps out, she

is "cheating" because it must mean something more than just sex. Perhaps she is purposely trying to punish her husband. It's almost expected for men to cheat at least once. Women on the other hand are expected to remain virtuous and loyal. Why is it when a man cheats he is a stud and when a woman cheats she is a whore?

4) Some men are threatened by career women. There are men who can't stand the idea of a woman being more successful than he is. If he is a traditionalist, true Madonna complex subscriber, then he may use women for sex as a way of some perverse form of retribution.

5) Most societies have different perceptions of divorce. Why is it that a divorced women with kids is most often considered used or damaged goods? Conversely, why is a divorced man considered "more seasoned" and "worldly"-- viewed with less stigma and sometimes more positively?

6) The Internet and technology have opened up so many new venues for people to engage in pornography, cyber sex and chat room affairs. Just because it is a virtual world and "unreal", most don't believe this is actual cheating/infidelity. Coincidentally, "most" who don't believe it, are men! There are more than one hundred million web pages devoted to pornography. It would be very interesting to correlate how many of these web pages have led to the downfall of relationships and marriages!

7) Men who possess the Madonna complex probably never get it right in a relationship until they make amends with and/or forgive their mothers. They first have to realize they are carrying with them a disdain toward women probably created by feeling unwanted, unloved and neglected by their mothers. It is never too late to forgive, even though you may never forget. A

man doesn't have to physically seek an apology from his mother nor does he have to be face to face to forgive her. He just needs to forgive, let go and move on!

8) We've discussed men who don't have sex with their wives because they are too busy watching porn and satisfying themselves that way. What about men who don't have sex with their wives or girlfriends because they are too bust watching sports or hanging out with their friends? Some women we spoke with asserted they felt they were constantly in competition with a man's best friends or sports for his attention and affection.

The standards for which we hold people accountable and perceivable in relationships will always be the same. They will always be based on truths, loyalties and consistency. People will always screw up and make mistakes when it comes to relationships -- it's in our nature to fail. Failures do not have to equate with failures, rather lessons learned. The sooner men with the Madonna complex realize they are a huge part of the problem and seek the help they need, and the sooner women enable these men by accepting their degrading whims instead of kicking them to the curb, the sooner will relationships get better, or more workable! It would appear when it comes to turning a blind eye toward cheating, infidelity and perversions, ignorance is bliss. It is more readily easy to opt for the blind eye approach.

REFERENCES

Bandura, A. (1960). Relationships of family patterns to child behavior disorders (Progress report, USPHS, Project No. M-1734). Stanford, CA: Stanford University.

Bandura, A., & Huston, A. (1961). Identification as a process of incidental learning. Journal of Abnormal and Social Psychology, 63 (12), 311-318.

Beck, A.T. (1991). Cognitive Therapy. American Psychologist, 46, 368-375.

Bem, S.L. (1983). Gender Schema theory and its implications for child development: Raising gender aschematic children in a gender-schematic society. Signs, 8, 598-616.

Berne, E. (1964). Games people play. New York: Grove Press.

Celani, D.P. (1994). The Illusion of Love: Why the Battered Woman Returns to her Abuser. Columbia University Press.

Cooley, C.H. (1922). Human Nature and the Social Order, rev. ed. New York: Scribner's.

Diagnostic and Statistical Manual of Mental Disorders, Fourth Edition (DSM-IV-TR) American Psychological Association 2002.

http://www.checkfacebook.com/

Freud, S. (1905). These essays on the theory of sexuality. In Standard edition, Vol. VII, pp. 125-245. London: Hogarth Press, 1953.

Freud, S, (1913). Totem and taboo. New York. Vintage Books.

Freud, S. (1943). A general introduction to psychoanalysis. Garden City, NY; Garden City Publishing. (Originally published 1971).

Freud, S. (1953). Contributions to the psychology of love: A special type of choice objects made by men. In E. Jones (Ed.), Collected papers (Vol. 4) (pp. 192-202). London; Hogarth Press. (Originally published 1933).

Gray, J. (1992). Men are from Mars, women are from Venus: A practical guide for improving communication and getting what you want in your relationship. Harper Collins Press.

Lamb, M.E. (1986). The father's role: Cross-cultural perspectives. Hillsdale NJ: Erlbaum.

Langlois, J.H., & Downs, A.C. (1980). Mothers, fathers, and peers as socialization agents of sex-typed play behaviors in young children. Child Development, 51, 1237-1247.

Parke, R.D., & O'Leary, S.E. (1976). Father-mother-infant interaction in the newborn period: Some findings, some observations and some unresolved issues. In K.F. Roegal & J.A. Meacham (Eds.) The developing individual in a changing world: Vol. 2. Social and environmental issues (pp. 653-663). Chicago: Aldine.

Piaget, J. (1952). The origins of intelligence in children. New York: International Universities Press.

Sacco, P.A. (2003). Why women want what they can't have. Bookman Publishing.

Sacco, P.A. & Schott, J. (2008). Penis Envy. Australia: Inkstone Press

Sacco, P.A. & Schott, J. (2007). Fast food dating, tour 2 cents. Booklocker Press

Walster, E., Walster, G.W., & Berscheid, E. (1978). Equity: Theory and research. Boston: Allyn and Bacon.

OTHER RECOMMENDED READINGS

Deborah Tannen
Gender And Discourse

John Gray
Mars And Venus Together Forever: Relationship Skills
    For Lasting Love

John Bradshaw
Creating Love/ The Next Stage Of Growth

Gloria Steinem
Revolution From Within: A Book Of Self-Esteem

Laura C. Schlessinger
Ten Stupid Things Couples Do To Mess Up Their
    Relationships

ABOUT THE AUTHORS

PETER ANDREW SACCO PH.D.

Peter is an international author of the popular selling books *What's Your Anger Type?* and Why Women Want What They Can't Have.... He is former TV talk show host of Mental Health Matters and resident expert on many TV shows. Helping clients manage their mental health issues for many years, Peter continues to offer lectures, seminars and classes in mental health issues, addictions and relationships. A psychology professor (specializing in addictions, relationships and criminal psychology) and former private practitioner, Peter resides in Niagara Falls, Canada. You can visit Peter at his website: www.petersacco.com

DEBRA LAINO D.H.S.

As a sex therapist and a mental health professional Debra sees clients with varying issues in her private practice; individual sexuality issues including desire disorders, orgasm disorders, arousal disorders, sex addiction, gender orientation issues and more. In addition she counsels couples dealing with relationship issues. Debra has also spent many years working in the mental health field dealing helping clients deal with depression, anxiety, compulsive behaviours, couples, etc. Her clients continue to influence her and help her to grow on a multitude of levels. As a young woman who has dealt with a desire disorder herself, she has great insight and empathy for clients going through these issues. Debra resides in the USA.

Lightning Source UK Ltd.
Milton Keynes UK
UKHW011935260122
397754UK00002B/572